Peter Gorton's HORN OF PLENTY

COOKERY BOOK

HALSGROVE

First published in Great Britain in 1996 by Halsgrove

British Library Cataloguing in Publication Data
A CIP Catalogue Record for this book is available from the British Library

ISBN 1 874448 05 1

HALSGROVE

Halsgrove House,
Lower Moor Way,
Tiverton,
Devon EX16 6SS
Tel: 01884 243242
Fax: 01884 243325

Printed and bound in Great Britain by The Cromwell Press, Wiltshire

CONTENTS

DEDICATION

This book is affectionately dedicated to my wife Kaz
for all her love, tolerance and support;
and to the memory of my late mother.

ACKNOWLEDGEMENTS

I would like to thank all the chefs I have worked with and everybody who has helped to make this book happen.

My special thanks go to Ian and Elaine Gatehouse for all their help and support over the past six years; to Margaret Jones for her untiring input and typing skills; and to Sarah Kennedy. Thanks also to Halsgrove, especially Charles Wood and Karen Binaccioni for all their hard work and patience.

Thanks also to all those companies who have helped in the production of this book and the accompanying videos. These include: Britannia Shellfish; Country Cheeses, N. H. Creber, The Fine Foods Company, Howells Butchers, Tony and Heather Jackson, Anne and Peter Woodliffe, and to Percy (fish supplier to The Horn of Plenty for thirty years).

Finally I would like to thank my team at The Horn of Plenty for their constructive comments and help.

NOTES

Here are a few notes and guidance to help you before you start on your kitchen adventure!

All ingredients should be weighed and prepared in advance.

'Chef's Tips' and notes are there to point out any difficulties and give you help and guidance.

Difficulty of recipes is indicated by the number of rosettes shown on the list of contents at the head of each chapter. One rosette means an easy dish, two rosettes slightly more complicated and three rosettes means the recipe is more advanced and may be lengthy.

Ovens vary considerably so adjust cooking times if needed.

Taste as you cook and adjust seasoning to your own personal taste.

Always buy the freshest ingredients available.

Finally, try to have a mental picture of the finished dish; with this in mind you should be able to see all the steps leading to it.

FOREWORD

I most certainly am not the only person rising from my downy bed at 4am weekday mornings. By Friday night, and after a long journey, the joy and comfort that Peter's cooking at The Horn of Plenty brought to me - along with a group of good friends – ah it was heaven! Double heaven at breakfast. What a treat: bacon, eggs, sausage, fried bread and the pleasure of my brother and sister-in-law's company AND a lovely long chat with Peter. He cares. He is a true fine-fingered professional with a natural magic for food.

He'll go far – and I'll be following!

Sarah Kennedy

AUTHOR'S INTRODUCTION

I love eating good food – to me it is one of the great pleasures of life; whether it is an informal meal cooked at home with family and friends, or a culinary feast served in one of the finest restaurants in the world.

I have always considered myself lucky; not only is cooking my vocation it is also my favourite hobby. Through my years of cooking as a professional chef I have tried to marry natural ingredients one with another to find simple harmonies that enhance rather than overpower.

A recipe in my eyes is not meant to be followed exactly. Try adding the zest of this, a drop of that, or maybe a tiny pinch of spice. Let yourself be led by your palate and heart. I have always cooked to give pleasure and joy and to try to bring a closeness between the people I cook for and myself.

Cooking is a matter of interpretation, adaptability and creativity. I have collected many recipes over the years and have added my own personal international touch to this book. I have tried my best to make the recipes accessible to all cooks, and have attempted to limit the amount of 'hard to find' ingredients to a minimum. Various 'Chef's Tips' appear in this book to give guidance and to present information that should help you improve your cooking and teach you about unusual ingredients and techniques of modern international cooking.

I have had a wonderful time testing recipes with my chefs and cookery students and would like to encourage you to have fun with this book. Don't forget to mix and match recipes. Nothing replaces a 'hands-on' approach to cooking. The only way to improve is to experiment and make mistakes – I learn something different every day! So have a go and don't lose heart.

Finally, if you would like to cook successfully, freshness of ingredients is the key, followed by flavour, texture and presentation. So go ahead and take the plunge, you and whoever you share these recipes with will be delighted you did!

Happy cooking fellow chefs – off to your stoves!

STARTERS, APPETISERS OR HORS D'OEUVRES

The two strongest memories when you visit someone's house are usually the first impression as you arrive and your last impression as you leave. The same can be true of a meal, and because the starter or appetiser is the first course in a meal, it is essential that it should always create a good impression. It should be a light and appetising course, colourful in appearance and stimulating to the appetite.

The following recipes have been carefully selected to give a varied and interesting selection of modern international cuisine, some will be equally good as picnic and barbecue food, or served as finger food for cocktail parties. There are also some inspirational dishes for dinner parties, they can be made in advance so that you can spend more time with your guests.

RECIPES

ORIENTAL CHICKEN SALAD
SERVES 4

Having spent time working in Thailand, I find I have developed a great love for the food of that region. Here follows one of my favourite starters and one we serve often at The Horn of Plenty.

Ingredients

4 chicken breasts (with skin on)
half a cucumber
2 fresh chillies - seeded
  and cut into fine strips
6 shallots sliced thinly
1 large tbsp of ginger -
  cut into matchsticks
2 cloves of garlic (chopped fine)
55g chopped coriander

50ml lime juice
3 tbsps fish sauce
5 tsps sugar
half tsp salt
2 tbsps olive oil
55g chopped roasted
  peanuts
Iceberg lettuce

Preparation

Add the chicken breasts to a saucepan of boiling water then reduce the heat and simmer for 8 minutes. Take off the heat and let chicken rest in the cooking water for 20 minutes. Remove the chicken and discard the skin. With your hands pull the meat apart in shreds, about 1.5 inches long, set aside.

Peel and seed the cucumber, cut into matchsticks and add to the chicken. In another bowl add the chillies, shallots, ginger and garlic, toss with lime juice, fish sauce and other ingredients then add to the chicken and cucumber and mix thoroughly, stir in the coriander. Place on top of crisp Iceberg lettuce, sprinkle with chopped peanuts and serve.

CHEF'S TIP

When preparing chillies always wash your hands after handling. Do not put your hands anywhere near your eyes, it can be a very nasty experience!

Fish sauce is the basic flavour of Thai cooking and may be obtained in most supermarkets.

THAI SEAFOOD SALAD
SERVES 4

Ingredients

175g cooked mixed
  shellfish per person
  (mussels, scallops, crab claws)
2 hearts of Cos lettuce
1 heart curly endive
quarter of a cucumber
  cut into matchsticks
half-inch of ginger root
  cut into matchsticks

Thai Sauce
2 dried or fresh chillies (small)
1 tbsp sugar
juice and pulp of 1 lemon
3 tbsps Ca Sac (fish sauce)
3 tbsps water
1 bunch of coriander leaves
  (to taste)

Liquidize all of the sauce ingredients together and set aside.

Preparation

Mix the cooked seafood with the cucumber and ginger and serve on a bed of the picked mixed lettuce. Pour a little of the Thai sauce on top of the shellfish and serve.

CHEF'S TIP

This Thai sauce makes a very good dipping sauce served with deep-fried prawns, fish etc.

Fish sauce is a fundamental ingredient in nearly every dish in South East Asia, just as soy sauce is used in China and Japan.

Fish sauce keeps indefinitely on the shelf.

THAI PORK APPETISER

SERVES 6–8

*This is a lovely light summer starter and one
which is perfect for a buffet or barbecue*

Ingredients

725g minced pork
4 shallots (chopped)
4 cloves of garlic (finely chopped)
115g roasted peanuts or pinenuts (coarsely pounded)
55g granulated sugar
1 tbsp minced coriander stalks
1 tsp ground black pepper
2 red chillies, seeded and cut into slivers
2 segmented oranges
mint or coriander leaves for garnish
2 tbsps peanut oil or olive oil
Iceberg lettuce

Preparation

Heat the peanut or olive oil and fry the garlic, coriander, red
chillies and shallots in a saucepan. In a separate pan fry the
pork, salt, pepper and sugar and stir fry until the pork is cooked
through, when browned add to the shallots etc.

Stir in the peanuts or pinenuts and mix thoroughly. Place a
heaped teaspoon full of the Thai pork on a crisp leaf of Iceberg
lettuce; garnish with the orange segments and mint or
coriander.

CHEF'S TIP

*The pork and the
shallot mixture should be
cooked in separate frying
pans. This stops the
meat stewing. Make sure
the oil is hot before you
add the pork or you
will stew the meat.*

BEEF PATTIES COOKED IN SRI LANKAN PASTRY

MAKES 36 COCKTAIL SIZE PORTIONS

Make these tasty patties large or cocktail size.

Ingredients

1 slice of bacon
115g finely minced beef
2 tbsps butter
1 small onion
1 clove garlic (crushed)
2 tsps curry powder
1 tsp ground coriander
half tsp salt
large pinch black pepper and turmeric
1 fresh green chilli
2 tsps lime or lemon juice
1 medium-size potato (boiled)
2 tbsps coconut-milk (optional)
225g Sri Lankan pastry (see page 100)

Preparation

Dice the bacon very finely and fry with the beef in the butter until the beef changes colour. Add the very finely chopped onion and garlic and fry until soft. Add the curry powder, coriander, salt, pepper and turmeric and fry for 2 minutes.

Slit open the chilli, scrape out the seeds and chop the flesh very finely. Mix the chilli, lemon juice and finely chopped potato and coconut-milk (if used) and simmer until the mixture is thick and dry.

Roll out the pastry very thinly. Cut out 36 rounds and place a small spoonful of the filling in the centre of each. Run a wet finger around the edge of the pastry and fold over, pinching the edges firmly to make the patty. Deep fry in hot oil or bake in a pre-heated oven 190°C (375°F, Gas Mark 5) until golden brown. Serve with a spicy dipping sauce.

CHEF'S TIP

If you make cocktail size patties, you can freeze them. When your guests arrive pop them in the oven, they will take 5 minutes to cook. Serve with your pre-dinner drinks

PAN-FRIED SCALLOPS WITH ASPARAGUS TEMPURA ON A POTATO DRESSING

SERVES 4

Ingredients

4 scallops
4 asparagus spears

Potato Dressing
200g potatoes
half a rasher of bacon
1 shallot
80ml chicken stock
1 tbsp Soy sauce
3 tbsps olive oil
1 tbsp red wine vinegar
salt
milled pepper
sprigs of tarragon, chervil and coriander
Tempura batter (see page 99)

Tempura batter (see page 99)

Preparation

Cook the potatoes in salted water until they are soft, cut the bacon in strips and chop the shallot. In a shallow pan heat the olive oil and add the bacon and the shallot and fry them, constantly stirring until they are slightly browned. Transfer to a mixing bowl. When the potatoes are cooked finely grate them on to the bacon and shallot. Heat the stock and add it together with the vinegar and Soy sauce. Season with salt and pepper and mix until it becomes smooth. Sauté the scallops for 2 minutes until golden on one side. Fry the blanched asparagus in the batter.

Presentation

Divide the warm potato dressing equally on pre-heated dinner plates. Arrange the scallops and tempura asparagus on top and add the fresh herbs.

CHEF'S TIP

Scallops should be an off-white colour and firm to the touch; dry scallops before cooking them, this stops any excess water coming out and stewing rather frying them. Do not overcook scallops, they so easily become tough and rubbery.

CHICKEN SATÉ WITH PESTO
MAKES 24 SKEWERS

Satés are ideal to be made a day in advance, then grilled,
pan-fried or baked as your guests arrive.

Ingredients

280g chicken breast
pesto sauce (see page 137)

Marinade
half a tsp cumin
1 tsp curry powder
2 tbsps olive oil
salt and freshly ground black pepper

Preparation

Cut the chicken breast into twenty-four 3x1-inch pieces. Place a skewer into each chicken piece, lengthways and arrange on a baking tray.

Now prepare the marinade; add all the above ingredients together and sprinkle over the chicken skewers making sure they are all well coated. Refrigerate for 1 hour.

Pre-heat your grill, arrange the skewers of chicken under the grill and top with one teaspoonful of pesto sauce. Grill until pesto is lightly browned, about 4 minutes.

Arrange the skewers on a platter and serve immediately with drinks.

CHEF'S TIP

You can make up a number of different skewers using pork, scallops, salmon, etc. I suggest coating them in breadcrumbs and then panfrying

ONION TART WITH BAKED RED PEPPERS

SERVES 4

Ingredients

Pastry
100g plain flour
50g butter, chopped
pinch of salt
cold water to mix

Filling
1 tbsp olive oil
2 large onions, thinly sliced
half tsp freshly grated
  nutmeg
1 tbsp plain flour
120ml double cream
2 eggs, size 3, lightly beaten
2 tbsps grated Parmesan
  cheese

Baked Peppers (see page 95)

Preparation

Pre-heat the oven to 200°C (400°F, Gas Mark 6). Grease a 15cm (6-inch) tart tin. Place the flour and butter in a bowl and, using your fingertips, rub the butter into the flour until it resembles fine bread-crumbs. Add salt. Then add about 3-4 tablespoons cold water, stirring gradually, until the mixture forms a firm dough. Wrap and chill for 15 minutes.

Prepare the filling by heating the olive oil in a saucepan, add the onions and cook for 10 minutes, covered, until softened and trans-parent. Remove the lid and cook for a further 5 minutes until golden. Season. Stir in the nutmeg, cheese and flour. Remove from the heat and stir in the cream and eggs.

Roll out the pastry on a lightly floured surface and use to line the base and sides of the tart tin, trimming away any excess. Prick the pastry base with a fork then pour in the onion mixture. Bake for 35–40 minutes until the top is golden.

A slice of the warm tart should be served with half a pepper and a little seasonal salad.

QUICHE OF AVOCADO AND SMOKED SALMON TROUT

SERVES 4

Ingredients

Filling
1 avocado
200g smoked salmon trout, or
  prawns, lobster etc
200ml cream
200ml milk
3 eggs
salt and freshly ground pepper
dash of nutmeg

Pastry
250g plain flour
180g butter
pinch of salt
1 egg
water

Preparation

Work flour, butter and salt together until it becomes 'sandy' in texture. Add the egg and a few tablespoons of water, one at a time until the dough forms a ball. Wrap in clingfilm and refrigerate for a few hours.

Grease a 15cm (6-inch) tart tin. Roll out the pastry on a lightly floured surface and use to line the tart tin, trimming away any excess. Bake the pastry blind with foil and dried beans. Place in a pre-heated oven 180°C (350°F, Gas Mark 4) for 30 minutes, remove from the oven, allow to cool, remove the dried beans and foil.

Prepare the filling, peel and stone the avocado and cut into small cubes. Cut the salmon trout into strips. Place salmon and avocado in the pre-baked tart mould. Put the cream, milk, eggs and seasoning into a blender and liquidize for a few seconds. Pour evenly over the salmon and avocados. Return to the oven and switch off the oven and let the quiche cook for about 1 hour in a cooling oven.

Serve warm with a seasonal salad of your choice.

CHEF'S TIP

Dried beans or kidney beans can be used, or you can buy dried beans or metal pie weights from a cake shop or cookware shop.

CRAB AND PRAWNS IN FILLO PASTRY WITH A RED PEPPER SAUCE

SERVES 4

This is a wonderful starter and a real crowd pleaser, yet is very easy to make and can be made a day in advance.

Ingredients

450g cooked prawns and white crab
  meat mixed
2 tbsps unsalted butter
2 cloves garlic
half tsp ground cumin
three-quarter to 1 tsp cayenne pepper

half tsp paprika
4 tsps plain flour
225ml double cream
2 tbsps chopped herbs
salt and pepper
tsp grated lemon zest

Red Pepper Sauce
55g unsalted butter
1 small red pepper, cored, seeded and diced
2 shallots diced
2 cloves garlic, mashed
175g flat mushrooms, roughly chopped
150ml white wine
150ml water
4 tbsps double cream
passata (to taste)
lemon juice
salt and freshly ground white pepper

Preparation

Melt 2 tablespoons butter in a medium saucepan over a low heat. Add the garlic and spices and cook for 1–2 minutes. Add the flour and stir well. Cook for another minute, then stir in the cream and cook until thickened. Remove from the heat and stir in the shellfish, fresh herbs, lemon zest, salt and pepper to taste. Cool.

Cut the fillo into strips 12x3 inches. To assemble, brush a strip of fillo pastry with melted butter. Top it with another strip and repeat again. Place a good tablespoon of the filling on to each strip. Fold the four sides of the fillo dough around the filling to make a purse shape.

Bake the fillo parcels on a baking sheet at 190°C (375°F, Gas Mark 5) until puffed and golden, about 7 minutes.

Red Pepper Sauce
In a small saucepan, melt the butter, sauté the pepper, onion and garlic until the onion is translucent, add the mushrooms and cook for another 10 minutes. De-glaze with the wine and cook until the wine has reduced by half. Add the water and cook for 5 minutes. Scrape the contents into a blender and purée until smooth. Strain, return to a clean pan, and re-heat. Add the double cream and some lemon juice, season to taste.

Pour the red pepper sauce on 4 pre-heated dinner plates arrange 3 fillo parcels on each plate and serve. Garnish with a light salad.

> ### CHEF'S TIP
>
> *Passata is puréed tomato and it is an ideal addition to sauces and soups.*

GOAT'S CHEESE AND BLACK OLIVES IN FILLO PASTRY

MAKES 36 CANAPÉ BITES

*These goat's cheese pastries can be served as a starter
or as canapés with drinks.*

Ingredients

3 sheets of fillo dough
175g fresh goat's cheese
280g finely chopped pitted olives
half tsp chopped thyme
freshly ground white pepper
a little melted butter

Preparation

In a small bowl, combine the goat's cheese, olives, thyme and
pepper to taste. Mix well and correct seasoning to taste.

Lay out one fillo sheet and brush lightly with melted butter.
Lay the second sheet directly on top and again brush with
butter. Repeat with the third sheet. Cut into 36 squares and
mound the cheese in the centre. Fold into triangles and brush
with melted butter. Bake until golden brown.

CHEF'S TIP

*I often serve these little
fillo purses in a seasonal
salad, hidden under
various leaves as a
suprise for my customers.*

MOUSSELINE OF SALMON SERVED WITH A HERB HOLLANDAISE

SERVES 4

Ingredients

150g fresh salmon
1 level tsp salt
large pinch of cayenne pepper
1 egg white
200ml to 350ml cream
1 quantity of herb hollandaise (see page 129)
a little butter

Preparation

Make sure the salmon and cream is well chilled. Purée salmon in a food processor, then add salt, pepper and egg white. Continue to purée for a few more seconds. Put the prepared mixture in a stainless steel bowl and chill. Stand the bowl on ice and using a wooden spatula, incorporate the cream little by little. Return to the fridge. Using a fine mesh sieve and a plastic scraper, force through only a small amount of the mixture at a time. The mixture should be light and creamy.

Butter the insides of 4 moulds lightly. Use a deep roasting pan lined with greaseproof paper to protect the mousse from the heat from underneath. Pour in enough hot water to come at least three-quarters way up the sides of the moulds. Cover the moulds with foil. Cook the mousse in the oven at 160-170°C (325°F, Gas Mark 3). Timings may vary accordingly to the thickness of the moulds, quantities being made, etc.

Unmould the mousselines on to 4 pre-heated dinner plates, place a spoonful of herb hollandaise over the top of mousseline and glaze under the grill for 1 minute. Serve immediately.

CHEF'S TIP

For a lovely fish dish. Add some fresh chopped dill to the mousseline and place on a fillet of sole. Wrap the sole, with the mousse filling in it, in clingfilm and steam for 10 minutes; remove the clingfilm and serve.

ROASTED PIGEON ON POTATO LEEK PANCAKES WITH A PORT SAUCE

SERVES 4

Ingredients

2 pigeons
2 tbsps oil
salt and pepper

Potato Leek Pancakes
400g potatoes
100g leeks, cleaned
2 eggs, lightly beaten
1 small onion, peeled
salt
freshly ground black pepper
pinch nutmeg
150ml oil
  (to make the pancakes)

Sauce
2 shallots, finely chopped
40ml port
100ml red wine
100ml chicken or veal stock
100g butter
1 sprig thyme
salt and pepper
20g butter

Preparation

Potato and Leek Pancakes

Grate the potatoes into a bowl and rest for 5 minutes. Take out the potato and squeeze out all the water. Transfer potatoes into a clean bowl. Add the eggs, mix well and grate the onion into the mixture. Cut the leeks into very thin strips and blanch them in salted water. Refresh, drain and add to the potato mixture. Season with salt, pepper and a pinch of nutmeg.

Heat the oil in a large frying pan and place four portions of the potato mixture into the hot oil with a ladle, then spreading the mixture. Cook on both sides until the pancakes are brown and very crisp. Put them on a tray lined with a tea towel to keep warm.

Pigeon

Season the pigeons with salt and pepper. Heat the oil and seal the pigeons and cook in a pre-heated oven at 200–220°C (400–425°F, Gas Mark 6–7) for 10 minutes. Remove from the oven and allow to rest.

Port Sauce
In a small saucepan, melt 20g butter, add the shallots and sweat for 2 minutes. Add the port and red wine and reduce by half. Add the thyme and veal or chicken stock, reduce by half. Pass the sauce through a fine sieve. Bring the sauce to the boil, add salt and pepper and butter. Keep warm. Remove the breasts from the pigeons and add the bones from the pigeons to the sauce and allow to infuse for 5 minutes.

Place the potato leek pancakes in the centre of pre-heated dinner plates and arrange the sliced pigeon on top. Pour the hot sauce over the pigeon breasts and serve.

SMOKED SALMON RAVIOLI
WITH A LEMON
AND DILL SAUCE
SERVES 4–6 PEOPLE

Ingredients

115g smoked salmon, cut into 1 inch pieces
115g fresh salmon, cut into 1 inch pieces
1 tbsp chopped fresh dill leaves
1 egg
225ml whipping cream
salt and white pepper to taste

350g of plain pasta dough (see page 98)
1 egg, lightly beaten for an egg wash

Sauce

100ml dry white wine
50ml Vermouth
salt and freshly ground white pepper
1 tbsp chopped dill

100ml fish stock (optional)
200ml double cream
juice of half a lemon
tbsp olive oil

Preparation

To prepare the mousse. Add the smoked salmon and fresh salmon to a food processor, blend until a light paste consistency. Add the chopped dill and the egg, mix for a few seconds, then add the cream with the machine running, pouring through the feed tube, process until the mixture is smooth. Transfer to a small chilled bowl and season with salt and pepper. If the mousse is too thick fold in a little more cream and refrigerate until needed.

Cut the pasta dough into 4 pieces using one piece at a time. On a floured surface using a pasta machine or by hand, roll out the first piece of dough to a rectangle about 30 inches long and 6 inches wide, brush with egg wash and using a half a tablespoon of the mousse, place 16 mounds on the dough in two rows each about 1 inch apart. Roll out the second piece of dough and cover, pressing down around the moulds to expel any air and seal. With a sharp knife or pastry cutter, cut into the desired shape. Arrange on a tray dusted with flour. Repeat with remaining dough. Refrigerate until needed.

Lemon and Dill Sauce

Reduce the white wine and Vermouth by half, add the fish stock, if used, and reduce by half. Add the cream and reduce again until it becomes lightly thick, add the lemon juice, season with salt and freshly ground pepper, add the finely chopped dill.

Bring a large pot of water to the boil with a tablespoon of olive oil and add a little salt, cook the ravioli's for 5 minutes. Drain on a clean tea towel.

Divide the ravioli among 4 or 6 pre-heated dinner plates, spoon the sauce over and serve.

CRAB CAKES WITH CORIANDER AND PEPPERS SERVED WITH A RED PEPPER SAUCE

SERVES 4

This recipe brings back memories of the time I was filming a video on a crab trawler. This was an exciting experience as the weather was very rough. If you enjoy crab as much as I do here is a recipe I think you will love.

Ingredients

25g butter
half tbsp mustard
350g white crab meat
1 large egg
chopped coriander
150ml double cream
115g dry breadcrumbs
1 small onion, finely diced

half tsp cayenne
half red pepper, finely diced
85g fresh breadcrumbs
1 tsp grated lemon zest
salt and freshly ground
  pepper to taste
125ml olive oil

1 quantity of red pepper sauce
  (see Italian red pepper soup recipe page 32)

Preparation

Melt the butter in a medium saucepan over a medium heat. Add the onions and peppers and cook for 5 minutes. Add the mustard and cream and reduce by half. Leave to cool. Add all the remaining ingredients except the dry breadcrumbs. Shape into 8 patties about half an inch thick. Coat each crab cake with dry breadcrumbs and refrigerate until needed. Heat olive oil in a large sauté pan over a medium heat. Add as many crab cakes as will fit and sauté until golden brown. Serve hot with a red pepper sauce and sautéed greens.

CHEF'S TIP

Use the best white crab meat you can buy and remember to check for shell which might have been missed by the fishmonger.

You can deep fry the crab cakes but you will need to coat them in flour and egg then breadcrumbs.

24

MARINATED BREAST OF DUCK ON A SPICY LENTIL SALAD

SERVES 4

Ingredients

2 Breasts of marinated duck (see page 73)

Lentil Salad
200g lentils cooked
1 medium carrot
1 small leek
1 red pepper
3 tbsps olive oil
2 tbsps white wine vinegar
salt and freshly ground black pepper

Preparation

Wash and clean the leek, carrot and red pepper and cut them in very fine strips. Prepare the vinaigrette with olive oil and vinegar, salt and pepper. Add together the chopped vegetables, cooked lentils and vinaigrette.

Remove the duck breasts from the marinade, drain well. Pan-fry carefully on each side for 1 minute. Cook in the oven for about 4 minutes 200°C (400°F Gas Mark 6), remove and allow to rest.

Presentation

Arrange the lentil salad on dinner plates, cut the breasts in slices and place equal slices on the top of the salad (the breast should still be warm).

DEEP-FRIED MUSHROOMS WITH A HAM AND CHEESE FILLING

SERVES 6

Ingredients

12 large field mushrooms
225g Cheddar cheese
4 slices of bread (made into crumbs)
4 slices of ham, diced
1 small onion, finely chopped
1 carrot, finely chopped
2 celery sticks, finely chopped
2 garlic cloves, finely chopped
125ml white wine
1 tbsp chopped fresh herbs – parsley, tarragon, chives.

Coating
225g dried breadcrumbs or plain breadsticks
2 whole eggs, lightly beaten

Preparation

Sauté the chopped vegetables, add white wine and reduce until dry, add the cheese, breadcrumbs, fresh herbs and ham. Mix well and leave to cool.

Remove the stems from the mushrooms and press the filling into the cups. Dip into egg and then breadcrumbs. Deep-fry until golden brown, drain well and serve with a seasonal salad or with a spicy Aioli.

CHEF'S TIP

Sometimes this mixture will fill more mushrooms, make sure the mixture is dry and the mushrooms are well coated in breadcrumbs so that the filling does not explode while cooking.
If the ham is left out, this recipe makes a lovely vegetarian starter.

FISH RISOTTO WITH CRISP GINGER

SERVES 4

Ingredients

450g fresh white fish, cut into 1 inch pieces
55g fresh ginger, peeled and cut into julienne
80ml olive oil
4 garlic cloves, minced
225g onion or shallots, chopped fine
450g Arborio rice
1 medium tomato, chopped
115g Parmesan cheese
3 tbsps chopped parsley
225ml dry white wine
1.2ltr fish stock
fresh fried ginger for garnish (see below)

Preparation

In a medium saucepan, heat the olive oil. Over a medium-high heat, sauté the onion and the garlic until soft. Add the rice and continue to stir with a wooden spoon, coating the rice with the oil and the onion. Deglaze with the wine and cook until the liquid is absorbed, stirring often. Pour in enough fish stock to cover. Cook, stirring often until the liquid is absorbed. Spread the mixture over a baking sheet to cool until serving time.

Meanwhile, cook your selection of fish under the grill.

Pour 125ml of stock into the rice; turn the flame to high and stir in some salt and the tomatoes. Keep stirring. When it is the right consistency, add 55g of grated Parmesan cheese into the risotto. Add some parsley and check seasoning.

To fry ginger, heat oil in a medium saucepan to 180°C (350°F), fry until golden brown, about 3 minutes, drain and reserve.

Divide the risotto among 4 large dinner plates. Sprinkle with fried ginger and serve.

CHEF'S TIP

Arborio rice is a round-grained type of rice and its texture makes it ideal for risottos.

27

TAGLIATELLE OF ASPARAGUS, WILD MUSHROOMS AND FRENCH BEANS, WITH A SAFFRON CREAM

SERVES 4

Ingredients

1 recipe egg pasta (see page 98)
450g asparagus
450g French beans
225g – 450g wild mushrooms
chervil or chives, roughly chopped
grated Parmesan

few threads of saffron
350ml single cream
1 tbsp butter
2 shallots, finely chopped
1 thin strip of lemon peel,
   finely sliced
salt and pepper

Preparation

Cover the saffron with a couple of tablespoons of boiling water to make an infusion. Melt the butter in a wide sauté pan, gently cook the shallots for several minutes until soft. Fry the wild mushrooms. Add the cream and saffron infusion, bring to the boil and reduce slightly. Season with salt.

When the pasta water is boiling, add the salt and cook the asparagus, drain. Cook the beans and drain. Add both to the cream. Cook the pasta, when done add to the cream turning it over several times to coat with the sauce. Add the chervil leaves and lemon peel.

Serve on warm dinner plates with grated Parmesan.

SOUPS

There are soups suited to every occasion and to every season. Soups are especially helpful for the home cook since they are almost always made in advance. Certain soups like the red pepper, mushroom and tomato can also be used as sauces with the addition of a little cream and butter. Soups should be made with good ingredients and be prepared with the same attention to detail as all the other courses on your menu. Soups are versatile: try changing the garnishes and you will be able to create many new variations.

RECIPES

CHICKEN AND COCONUT-MILK SOUP
SERVES 6–8

A south-east Asian soup that is simple to prepare, and very tasty

Ingredients

1.2 ltrs thin coconut-milk
1 small chicken cut into bite-size pieces
2 stalks of lemon grass
2 chillies
3 spring onions, finely chopped
3 tbsps coriander leaves – chopped
juice of 2 limes
3 tbsps of fish sauce (Ca Sac)
600ml chicken stock (optional)

Preparation

Bring the coconut-milk to the boil and add the chicken pieces and lemon grass. Reduce the heat and simmer until the chicken is tender – about 15 minutes. Do not cover as this may make the coconut curdle. Add the spring onion, coriander leaves and chillies and bring the soup to just below boiling point. Stir in the lime juice and fish sauce, taste for seasoning and serve.

Fish or shell fish may be used instead of chicken. Noodles may also be added to the soup.

CHEF'S TIP

Fish sauce is added to nearly every dish in south-east Asia, just as soy is the most widely used sauce in China and Japan. Fish sauce keeps indefinitely, is inexpensive to buy and is available in most supermarkets.

FISH SOUP
SERVES 8–10

Ingredients

5 tbsps of olive oil
1.5 tbsps of clarified butter (see page 100)
6 garlic cloves
85g each of diced fennel, carrots, onions, leeks and celery
300ml white wine
150ml red wine
50ml brandy
225ml tinned Italian tomatoes
225ml passata
1 tbsp each of tarragon, basil, thyme and parsley
2 bay leaves
900g of mixed fish cut into pieces
2ltrs of water
1 tsp of ground saffron
pinch of cayenne pepper

Preparation

Heat the olive oil and clarified butter in a large pan. Fry the garlic and diced vegetables until golden then add the mixed fish and the red and white wine. Cook for a few minutes to allow the alcohol to evaporate then add the tomatoes, tomato purée and mixed herbs. Cook for 5 minutes then add the water and simmer for 1 hour. Liquidize the soup in batches and pass through a sieve squeezing out all the liquid, re-heat the soup add brandy and season to taste. Serve with Aioli.

CHEF'S TIP

This recipe may be made very economically if you buy fish trimmings or save and freeze fish trimmings when using fish for other purposes.

ITALIAN RED PEPPER SOUP
SERVES 6–8

Ingredients

6 tbsps of unsalted butter or olive oil
2 medium onions, sliced
4 garlic cloves
2 chillies
2 cloves
4 red peppers – about 450g
450g of ripe tomatoes or passata
2 bay leaves
2 sprigs of thyme
grated lemon zest or pesto (see page 137)
6 tbsps whipped cream
water

Preparation

Remove stems, seeds and veins from the chillies and cut the flesh into a few large pieces. Cover them with water, bring to the boil and simmer for 10 minutes. Slowly warm the olive oil or butter in a large pan with the herbs and cloves until they are aromatic, add the garlic, onions, peppers and salt, cook and stir well over a low heat until the vegetables are coated with olive oil. Add the tomatoes, chillies and water until it covers the peppers by an inch. Cook as slowly as possible.

Let the soup cool slightly then purée in a blender. Return soup to the saucepan season to taste with salt or chilli. Serve with chopped basil and a tablespoon of whipped cream flavoured with grated lemon zest or a spoonful of pesto.

CHEF'S TIP

This soup is also wonderful used as a sauce for pasta, or with a vegetarian dish.

PARSNIP SOUP
WITH CURRIED SPICES
SERVES 6

Ingredients

3–4 parsnips – about 7 inches long
4 tbsps of clarified butter (see page 100)
1 onion cut in small squares
1 tbsp curry powder
4 tbsps chopped coriander leaves
2–3 leeks (white parts only)
225g chopped carrots (peeled and diced) and 2 celery (diced)
1 tsp salt
1.2 ltrs stock or water
300ml cream
whole coriander leaves for garnish
3 radishes very thinly sliced for garnish

Preparation

Peel the parsnips, quarter them lengthways and cut into pieces. Heat the clarified butter in a soup pot and add the onion. Cook over a medium heat stirring frequently for about 15 minutes. Stir in the curry powder and half the coriander, then add the parsnips, leeks, carrots, celery, salt and the stock. Bring to the boil, lower the heat, cover and cook until the vegetables are soft. Liquidize the soup, sieve and return the soup to the pot. Stir in the cream and season to taste.

Serve the soup garnished with the remaining chopped coriander leaves and a cluster of thinly sliced radishes in each bowl.

CHEF'S TIP

To maximise flavour in your soups, the vegetables used should be sautéed to release a more intense flavour before adding stock or water.

CHILLED CREAM OF AVOCADO SOUP
SERVES 6

This is a refreshing summer soup.

Ingredients

3 ripe avocados
3 medium ripe tomatoes
juice of 2 oranges
juice of 1 lemon
2 small cloves of garlic – peeled and cut up finely
600 ml chicken stock
200 ml double cream
salt
freshly ground pepper

Preparation

Place the tomatoes into boiling water for 30 seconds then into iced water. Remove the skin, cut into halves and remove the seeds. Cut the tomato flesh into quarters.

Cut the avocados in half, remove the stone and the skin. Put the flesh and chopped tomatoes into a liquidizer. Add the orange and lemon juice, garlic and chicken stock, blend until smooth. Remove and add the cream, season to taste.

Serve in chilled bowls with freshly chopped chives.

MUSHROOM SOUP WITH TOMATO AND VERMOUTH
SERVES 6–8

Ingredients

140g butter
2 sticks celery – diced
2 medium onions – diced
450g of English or mixed mushrooms
300ml passata
1.2 ltrs chicken stock, water or vegetable stock
6 tbsps red Martini (Vermouth)
salt and freshly ground pepper
chopped parsley
freshly grated Parmesan cheese

Preparation

Heat half the butter in a saucepan over a low heat. Add the onions
and celery and cook for 5 minutes. Melt the remaining butter in a
saucepan add the mushrooms and cook until most of the juices are
released. Add mushrooms and their juices to the onion mixture, stir
in the passata and stock. Simmer for 20 minutes. Stir in the Martini.
Season to taste.

Serve hot with chopped parsley and Parmesan cheese.

POTATO AND LEEK SOUP
WITH SMOKED TROUT
SERVES 4

This is an interesting and unusual soup which is almost a meal in itself.

Ingredients

1 smoked trout
300g potatoes – peeled and diced
4 small shallots – peeled and cut up
1 carrot – peeled and diced
2 leeks – peeled and diced
140g butter
1 litre water
1 ham bone
black pepper – freshly ground
100ml double cream
chopped chives

Preparation

In a large saucepan melt the butter, add the shallots, leeks and carrots and cook until soft. Add the potatoes, water and the ham bone. Season with pepper and simmer for 1 hour. Remove the ham bone.

Remove from the heat and pass through a liquidizer, strain the soup back into the saucepan bring to a gentle simmer then add the cream and adjust the seasoning.

Skin the smoked trout and remove all the bones. Cut into bite size pieces and warm under the grill. Place the trout into the warmed soup bowls and fill the bowls with soup. Sprinkle with chives.

HOT AND SOUR CRAB SOUP

SERVES 6

If you are feeling adventurous try this delicious soup.

Ingredients

10 shiitake mushrooms – cut into strips
1.2 ltrs chicken stock
3 spring onions – chopped
225g fresh spinach – roughly chopped
2 tbsps dry sherry (optional)
2 – 3 tbsps rice vinegar, to taste
1 tbsp Soy sauce
2 tbsps cornflour
600ml water
freshly ground black pepper to taste
3 drops sesame oil
225g cooked crabmeat picked over
pinch chilli powder

Preparation

Sauté the mushrooms. Bring the chicken stock to a gentle simmer. Add the mushrooms and their juices, 2 spring onions and the spinach, simmer for 5 minutes. Stir in the sherry, vinegar and Soy sauce. Mix the cornflour with a little water and stir into soup. Cook gently stirring constantly until slightly thickened. Remove from the heat. Add pepper, sesame oil and crabmeat. Stir well. Pour the soup into warmed soup bowls and garnish with spring onions and chilli to taste.

CHEF'S TIP

Rice vinegar may be obtained in most large supermarkets. Buy only fresh crabmeat, try it first as some crabmeat is air blasted from the shells and lacks flavour.

GARLIC SOUP WITH FRENCH BEANS
SERVES 5–6

Ingredients

0.5 kg French beans
1 leek, washed and sliced
1 onions – peeled and diced
2 baking potatoes – peeled and diced
2 carrots – peeled and diced
100g mushrooms
1–2 heads of garlic
1 tbsp olive oil
30g butter
2 sprigs fresh thyme
1litre vegetable stock or water (see page 150)
salt and freshly ground black pepper
single cream (optional)

Preparation

Top and tail the French beans, reserve a few for garnishing the top of the soup. Slice thinly, set aside, cut the remainder in half. Separate the garlic heads into cloves but do not peel.

Heat the oil in a large pan and then add the butter, when it has melted add the vegetables together with the thyme, cook until lightly brown. Add the stock and bring to the boil, reduce the heat and simmer for 30 minutes until the garlic can be crushed easily. Liquidize the soup and sieve into a clean pan. Season to taste, serve with the shredded beans which have been blanched in water. Garnish with a swirl of cream.

CHEF'S TIP

If you blanche garlic in water and then cook it, the garlic is easier to digest. You will still get the full flavour without any noticeable after-effects!

JERUSALEM ARTICHOKE
AND MUSHROOM SOUP
SERVES 6

Ingredients

25g butter
1 tbsp olive oil
0.5kg Jerusalem artichokes, peeled
250g field mushrooms, roughly chopped
1 litre chicken stock, or water (see page 148)
125ml white wine
salt and pepper
cream to your taste (optional)

Preparation

Heat the butter and oil in a baking dish, wash, peel and dry the artichokes and toss them in the butter and oil with the mushrooms, bake in a pre-heated oven at 180°C (350°F, Gas Mark 4) for about 45 minutes. Bring the chicken stock to the boil and add the wine and simmer for 10 minutes, add the artichoke mixture to the stock and cook for 40 minutes. Season with salt and pepper. Remove from the heat and pass through a liquidizer, strain the soup back into a saucepan, bring to a gentle simmer. Add the cream and adjust the seasoning to taste.

To serve, add a few chopped chives or a swirl of basil oil (see page 53).

CHEF'S TIP

Jerusalem Artichokes have a nutty taste and are cooked in the same way as potatoes, you do not have to roast the artichokes but I find this gives the soup a stronger taste

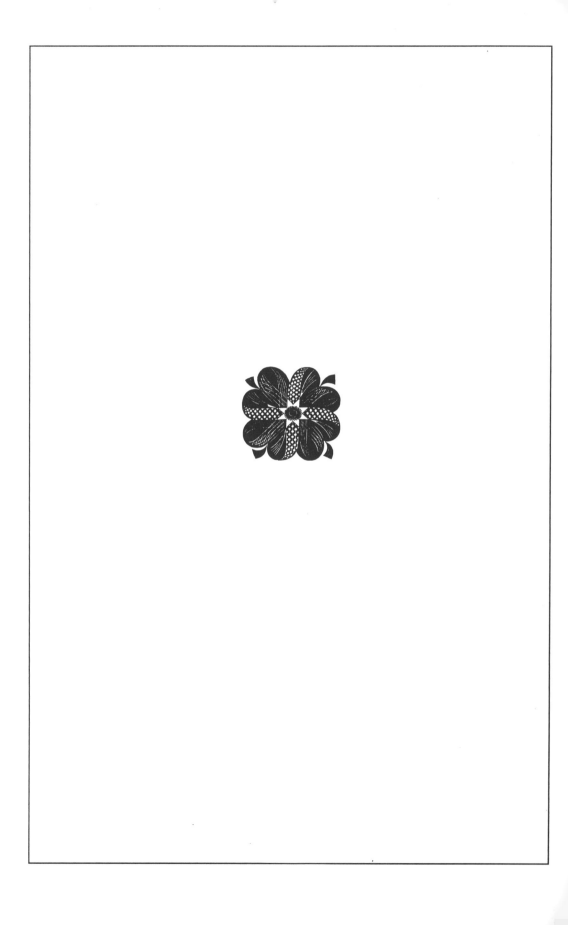

FISH AND SHELLFISH

What a great variety of excellent fish and shellfish there is around our shores. It would be unforgivable only to breadcrumb and deep-fry it and serve it with chips!

We have fish in all shapes and sizes, textures and colours. I love to experiment with fish and shellfish so I have included a few unusual ideas of preparing and serving them..

Remember, fish is juicier and tastes better when slightly underdone. When choosing fish, check that the fish smells of the sea, it should have no unpleasant odour and be bright, shiny and firm to the touch. The eyes are a very good indication of how fresh the fish is, they should be clear, bright and bulging.

Once you have bought your fish, it should be prepared and cooked as soon as possible. Fish deteriorates very quickly, only keep in the refrigerator for 2 days or in a deep-freeze for a few months.

RECIPES

GATEAUX OF FISH WITH A PRAWN SAUCE

SERVES 4

This is quite an expensive recipe but well worth the money when you see the look on your guests' faces when they try it.

Ingredients

225g puff pastry
700g sea bass, turbot, sole or salmon
225g spinach
225ml prawn sauce (see page 131)
225g lobster (diced for garnish) or prawns
25g unsalted butter
pinch of nutmeg

Preparation

Pre-heat oven 230°C (450°F, Gas Mark 8). Roll out the puff pastry as thinly as possible, place on a large baking tray and cook in the oven until crisp and golden, about 10 minutes. To prevent it from rising too much in the oven place a second baking tray on top; this will give a thin, crisp pastry. Using a pastry cutter cut out 4 circles about 3 inches in diameter, set aside.

Take four 65mm (2.5inch) diameter ramekins and butter well. Cook the spinach leaves in butter then season with salt, pepper and a touch of nutmeg. Cut the fish into equal slices and layer the bottom of a ramekin with salmon, then some spinach, then sole, more spinach, and finish with the turbot. Wrap in clingfilm and steam for 10 minutes, remove and allow to rest for 5 minutes. Cut the clingfilm and pour the juices into the prawn sauce.

Heat the prawn sauce, keep warm. Toss the lobster dice or prawns in a little butter. Season and set aside.

Presentation

Turn the gateaux out of the ramekin moulds on to 4 pre-heated dinner plates; arrange the lobster dice and pour the sauce around the gateaux. Brush the pastry lids with butter, heat up a metal skewer and mark the top of the pastry lid in a criss cross pattern, place on top of the gateaux and serve.

PAUPIETTES OF SOLE STUFFED WITH CRAB AND SERVED WITH A PRAWN SAUCE

SERVES 4

This dish can be made well in advance and is a lovely dish for that special dinner party.

Ingredients

4 medium size double fillets
  lemon sole
4 tbsps of fresh white crab meat
2 tbsps double cream
pinch of cayenne pepper
lemon juice to taste
salt and pepper
diced tomato
chopped chives

Sauce
Prawn sauce (see page 131)

Preparation

Mix together the crab meat, cream and cayenne pepper. Season with lemon juice, salt and pepper. Place a tablespoon of the crab mixture between each double fillet of lemon sole. Wrap in clingfilm. Place in a steamer and cook for 10 minutes

Presentation

When the sole is cooked, place on pre-heated plates, warm the prawn sauce and pour over the sole. Sprinkle with diced tomato and chives

CHEF'S TIP

The prawn sauce recipe will make more than four servings so freeze what's left into plastic cups, so when you need an instant sauce just run the cup under the hot tap. Place in your pan and reduce slightly and add a little cream.

ASSORTED SEAFOOD AND CRUSTACEANS ON A CREAM OF SPINACH AND WATERCRESS SAUCE

SERVES 4

Use any fish or shellfish you like;
the ingredients shown here are just a guide.

Ingredients

150g lemon sole
150g salmon
150g whiting (red bream)
100g prawns
100g mussels

Sauce
100g spinach
1 bunch of watercress
400ml fish stock (retained after
    cooking fish and crustaceans)
100g double cream
salt
lemon juice
freshly ground pepper
50g butter
half an onion (finely chopped)
cup of white wine

Preparation

Seafood

Divide the fish fillets and prawns into 4 equal portions. Poach fish until cooked in fish stock. Retain fish stock for sauce.

Spinach and Watercress Sauce

Wash spinach and boil for a short time in salted water. Refresh and drain. Chop spinach coarsely. Wash and chop watercress. Put the spinach, watercress and half of the fish stock in a commercial blender. Sieve mixture through a fine sieve and add the cream to the mixture. Add salt, lemon juice and freshly ground pepper to taste.

Melt the butter in a saucepan, add chopped onion and sweat for a few seconds. Add the white wine and remaining fish stock and reduce by half. Add the cream mixture and bring to the boil. Adjust seasoning and add as much watercress and spinach mix to form a good sauce, adjust to taste, keep warm.

CHEF'S TIP

When buying shellfish make sure all the mussels, clams etc. are closed tightly. If they are not give them a tap, if they do not close, discard them as they are dead.

GRILLED MARINATED SALMON WITH AN ORANGE AND MINT AIOLI

SERVES 4

Ingredients

2 tbsps salt
55g sugar
2 tbsps grated orange zest
1 tsp ground pepper
4 salmon fillets – 175g–200g each

mixed lettuce of choice
salt and pepper

Baked peppers – (see page 95)

Aioli

2 large egg yolks
1 tbsp fresh lemon juice
olive oil
1 tbsp puréed garlic
3 tbsps fresh orange juice
2 tbsps grated orange zest
salt
2 tbsps ground black
  pepper
mint leaves to taste

Baked peppers – (see page 95)

> ## CHEF'S TIP
>
> *After the salmon has been marinated and you have washed off any excess salt you can put the salmon (diced) on kebab skewers and barbecue. The taste is wonderful.*

Preparation

Cure the salmon fillets, mix the salt, sugar, orange zest and pepper. Rub over both sides of the salmon fillets and refrigerate for about 2 hours. Wash salmon well and dry and refrigerate.

Aioli

Whisk the egg yolks and lemon juice in a mixing bowl. Gradually whisk or beat in the oil. The mixture should be thick and emulsified. Whisk in the garlic, three tablespoon of orange juice, the zest and pepper. Season to taste with salt. Refrigerate until ready to serve.

Method

Brush the salmon fillets with olive oil and grill until just cooked through about 2–3 minutes each side. Place on serving plates and top with a spoonful of the aiole. Garnish with the chopped roasted peppers mixed with the salad leaves and serve.

PAN-FRIED FILLETS OF SEA BASS WITH A CONFIT OF TOMATOES, ASPARAGUS AND CRISPY BASIL

SERVES 4

This is the starter dish I made for the Egon Ronay
Guide Chef of the Year competition.

Ingredients

4 fillets of sea bass
50g plain flour
4 tbsps olive oil

4 tbsps butter
25g star anise

Tomato Confit

4 medium tomatoes, peeled,
  de-seeded and quartered
olive oil

6 sprigs of thyme
salt and pepper
2 cloves of garlic

Asparagus and Crispy Basil

8 asparagus spears

12 basil leaves fried until crisp

Sauce

20g shallots finely chopped
30ml Vermouth
60g butter
200ml double cream

200ml fish stock
salt and pepper
150ml white wine
pinch of saffron

Preparation

Tomato Confit

Peel de-seeded and cut tomatoes into quarters place in an oven proof dish. Cover with olive oil and finely sliced garlic, add thyme and seasoning. Cook in a pre-heated oven for 40 minutes at 100°C (200°F, Gas Very Slow). Leave to cool.

Sauce

Melt the 10g butter and sweat the chopped shallots, add wine, Vermouth and fish stock, reduce by two-thirds. Add double cream and reduce by half again. Infuse the saffron and whisk in the butter. Season with salt and pepper, sieve and set aside.

Asparagus

Peel and cook asparagus in salted boiling water, refresh in iced water and set aside.

Crispy Basil

Cook basil in a deep fat fryer at 170°C degrees until crisp. Remove and place on kitchen paper. Season with salt and pepper.

Sea bass fillets

Heat oil and butter in a pan, cut and score bass skin in crosses and sprinkle a little star anise on to each fillet. Season with salt and pepper, dust with flour and fry carefully until golden brown on the skin side only. Place on kitchen paper to remove excess oil. Keep warm.

Presentation

Arrange warm asparagus on warm plates, place a fillet of seabass on top of the asparagus leaving the tips showing. Put the tomato confit and crispy basil on top of the bass and serve.

WHOLE FRIED FISH WITH GINGER SAUCE

SERVES 6–8

Ingredients

Sauce
10 English mushrooms sliced
4 tbsps rice wine vinegar
6 tbsps of brown sugar
150ml water
3 tbsps dark sweet Soy sauce
2 spring onions sliced finely
1 piece of fresh ginger chopped
juice of 1 lime
1 tbsp cornflour blended with
  4 tbsps cold water
chopped fresh chilli (optional)
coriander

Fish
1.36kg whole fresh white fish
  or 4 fillets cod (cleaned
  and scaled)
salt
900 ml of vegetable oil
1 quantity of tempura batter
  (see page 99)

Preparation

Sauce
Put the vinegar, sugar, water and Soy sauce together in a medium saucepan and bring to the boil, cook stirring for 5 minutes. Add the mushrooms, spring onions and ginger and stir until the onions are limp. Pour in the lime juice and stir once or twice. Introduce the cornflour and water a dash at a time, stirring rapidly until it blends and is uniform. The sauce should have a shiny appearance.

Fish
Heat the oil in your largest wok or frying pan until a thin haze of smoke starts to appear. Carefully place the fish into the batter and fry until crisp and golden – about 6 minutes. Immediately remove to a large dish, letting the excess oil drain away. Pour the sauce over the fish and garnish with the chilli, coriander and a fine slicing of spring onions. Serve the fish with stir fry vegetables.

CHEF'S TIP

Once you've tried fried fish in tempura batter you will never want to use any other batter. It is so light and does not absorb so much oil (see page 99)

BREADCRUMBED WHITING ON A WARM ANCHOVY VINAIGRETTE

SERVES 4

Ingredients
8 fillets of whiting (weighing approx. 120g each)
2 eggs
200g white breadcrumbs
salt and freshly ground black pepper
olive oil for pan-frying

Anchovy vinaigrette
1 boiled egg
2 tomatoes, peeled, seeds removed
  and sliced into small cubes
4 anchovy fillets
1 shallot
1 clove garlic, finely chopped
1 tbsp fresh herbs of your choice
salt and freshly ground
  black pepper
6 tbsps olive oil
1 tbsp tarragon vinegar

Preparation

Anchovy vinaigrette
Boil the egg for 10 minutes and refresh. Chop the shallot very finely and place in a saucepan; add the chopped garlic and the olive oil. Cook over a low heat, stirring until the shallot is soft. Remove from the heat, cool and add the vinegar. Dice the anchovy fillets and the boiled egg finely. Add the vinaigrette. Add the chopped fresh herbs and tomatoes. Set aside.

Whiting
Remove any bones from the whiting fillets. Lightly season with salt and pepper. Break the eggs into a shallow dish, add a tablespoon of oil and whisk. Dip each fillet of fish in the egg mixture and then cover both sides in the breadcrumbs. Fry them gently in the olive oil until golden brown and place them on kitchen paper to remove any excess oil. Keep warm.

Divide the anchovy vinaigrette evenly on 4 warm dinner plates. Arrange 2 fillets of whiting on each plate. Serve with creamy mashed potatoes (see page 90).

SAUTÉED HADDOCK WITH A CURRY SAUCE

SERVES 4

This dish is very good served with risotto and hard boiled quails eggs or just with plain boiled rice.

Ingredients

3 tomatoes, peeled, seeds removed and diced
50ml olive oil
4 shallots or 1 small onion, finely chopped
1 clove of garlic, finely chopped
1 tbsp of curry powder
1 pinch fresh finely diced chilli
125ml white wine
225ml double cream
1 tbsp flour
4 fillets of haddock, cut into 8 pieces
1 tbsp fresh parsley or tarragon
freshly ground white pepper, to taste

Preparation

Blanch the tomatoes in boiling water for 10 seconds, peel off the skin. Remove the seeds and chop the pulp in quarter-inch dice.

In a saucepan heat 1 tablespoon of olive oil, sauté the chopped shallots for 1 minute. Add the garlic, tomatoes, half of the curry powder, salt and pepper, chilli and white wine. Bring to the boil for 2 minutes. Stir in the cream, return to the boil and simmer for 15 minutes. Keep warm.

Mix the flour and remaining curry powder together, dust the fish on both sides. In a large frying pan, heat the rest of the olive oil, sauté the fish until it is golden on both sides, about 4 minutes each side. Spoon the sauce over the fish on 4 pre-heated dinner plates, sprinkle with chopped herbs and serve.

CHEF'S TIP

To seed tomatoes, cut them in half, hold half the tomato cut-side-down and squeeze the tomato gently. The seeds and some pulp will drop out quite easily.

50

BAKED TROUT WITH
A MUSSEL FILLING
SERVES 6

Ingredients

4 trout
2kg mussels, steamed and removed from their shells
100g breadcrumbs
125ml single cream
50g pinenuts
200g spinach, watercress or sorrel
4 anchovy fillets (diced)
a few threads saffron
salt and freshly ground pepper

Preparation

Clean the mussels and steam until the shells are open. Soak the breadcrumbs in the cream. Toast the pinenuts in the oven until golden brown, watch they do not burn. Steam the spinach or sorrel and chop roughly. Crush the pinenuts add to the spinach, mix in the breadcrumbs and the anchovy fillets. Remove the mussels from their shells and toss with the saffron, add to the mixture and mix well.

Bone the trout leaving on the head and tail. Have ready 6 sheets of foil large enough to encase the fish. Place a fish on each piece of foil. Inside each fish place a few tablespoons of the filling to form an envelope and place on a baking tray in a pre-heated oven 200°C (400°F, Gas Mark 6) for about 20 minutes or until the fish is just cooked.

ROASTED SALMON WITH MIXED PEPPERCORNS, GINGER AND GARLIC

SERVES 4

Ingredients

4 salmon fillets, weighing about 175g–200g each
salt
25g unsalted butter
1 tbsp olive oil
1.5 tbsp crushed mixed peppercorns
1.5 tbsp chopped fresh ginger (peeled)
2 cloves garlic, chopped finely

Preparation

Season the salmon lightly with salt, brush the top with a little melted butter, Immediately sprinkle evenly with crushed mixed peppercorns and ginger and chopped garlic. Drizzle the remaining butter over the fillets. Refrigerate covered until needed

Pre-heat the oven to 250°C (500°F, Gas Mark 10), brush some olive oil over a baking tray large enough to hold the salmon. Roast for 10 minutes, the salmon should be cooked on the outside but still be moist and slightly underdone on the inside.

Serve with stir-fried cabbage with shiitake mushrooms (see page 86)

PAN-FRIED FILLET
OF SEA BREAM
(SKIN ON)
SERVES 4

Ingredients

4x140g pieces red bream (skin on)
salt and pepper
2 tbsps olive oil
115g sun-dried tomatoes, soaked in hot water, drained
  and julienned
2 garlic cloves, finely minced
2 tbsps chopped fresh parsley
4 tbsps shallots
4 tsps basil oil

CHEF'S TIP

*Sun-dried tomatoes need
to be soaked in hot water
for about 20 minutes.
This makes them soft
and usable*

Preparation

Season the red bream fillets with salt and pepper. Pre-heat a
sauté pan with the olive oil until hot. Add the sea bream to the
hot pan and cook flesh-side down for 4–5 minutes over a
medium heat. Turn to cook the skin side an additional 3
minutes until the skin is crispy.

Lift bream with a slotted spatula, leaving the juices and oil in
the pan. Add the sun-dried tomatoes, garlic and shallots, and
sauté together for 2 minutes. Add the fresh herbs to the pan.
Stir quickly, just to heat the herbs. Pour the sun-dried tomato
and herb mixture over the red bream then drizzle 1 teaspoon of
basil oil over each fillet and around the dish.

Basil oil
Blanch basil leaves in boiling water. Refresh and add some
olive oil in a blender. Strain the oil and allow to rest in the
fridge.

DEEP-FRIED MUSSELS WITH VEGETABLE NOODLES

SERVES 4

*This recipe is light and the crisp strips of vegetables make
a colourful accompaniment to the mussels.*

Ingredients

4 dozen mussels
4 tbsps olive oil
1 tbsp chopped parsley and dill
juice of half lemon
freshly ground white pepper
50g melted butter
200g white breadcrumbs
200g clarified butter

Vegetable noodles
500g packet of fresh noodles
1 small leek, cut into fine strips 3-4mm wide
1 small carrot, cut into fine strips 3-4mm wide
1 red pepper, cut into fine strips 3-4mm wide
50g butter
salt and freshly ground white pepper

Preparation

Scrape and wash the mussels, cook them until opened: they are
cooked when they open. Discard any mussels that don't open.
Remove from the heat and take out of the shells, cool, then marinate
in lemon juice, olive oil, chopped parsley and seasoning. Take the
mussels out of the marinade and pat dry, dip them in melted butter
then in the fresh breadcrumbs and set aside.

Vegetable noodles
Blanch the vegetable sticks in boiling salted water for about 2 minutes. Refresh and drain. To finish the noodles in lots of boiling water
cook them al dente. Refresh and drain, melt the butter in a large pan
add the vegetable strips and noodles, stir well and warm through.
Season with salt.

Mussels
Add a few at a time to the clarified butter and fry until golden brown, drain them on a tray lined with kitchen paper. (To clarify butter melt butter over a moderate heat until all the water has evaporated, don't brown, pour the butter through a cheese-cloth into a frying pan.)

Divide the noodles on to the centre of 4 pre-heated dinner plates. Arrange the hot mussels in a circle around the vegetables and sprinkle with sprigs of fresh herbs or a sauce of your choice (red pepper sauce goes very well).

SESAME FRIED SCALLOPS WITH GINGER AND ROASTED RED PEPPER VINAIGRETTE

SERVES 4

Ingredients

Marinade

3 large egg whites
55g Soy sauce
2 tbsps sesame oil
1 tbsp fresh ginger
2 finely chopped shallots
   or 1 small onion
20 scallops,
   side muscle removed
8 tbsps sesame seeds
50ml olive oil

Ginger and Pepper Vinaigrette

1tbsp finely chopped fresh ginger
1 sweet red pepper, roasted, peeled
   and seeded and chopped finely
1tbsp fresh herbs of your choice
2 tbsps finely chopped shallots
2 tbsps pitted and chopped black
   olives
50ml balsamic vinegar
225ml olive oil
salt and freshly ground pepper

Preparation

Pre-heat oven to 180°C (350°F, Gas Mark 4). Combine all the ingredients for the marinade together, whisk lightly until frothy. Add the scallops and marinate for 30 minutes. Drain the excess liquid off the scallops and dip them in the sesame seed coating, covering them completely on all sides. Keep in a refrigerator for 20 minutes.

Whisk the salt and pepper into the olive oil slowly so that the mixture will emulsify together, add all the ingredients for the red pepper vinaigrette. This quantity will make 400ml of dressing; refrigerate and it will keep for a week.

Heat the olive oil in a large frying pan and sauté the scallops on each side until crisp. Transfer to an oven tray and place in the oven for 2 minutes.

Place some sautéed spinach or stir-fried vegetables (see page 85) in the centre of 4 pre-heated dinner plates. Pour some of the vinaigrette around and place the scallops around the vegetables. Serve immediately.

CHEF'S TIP

There are a number of ways to roast peppers, this is the one I have found to be most successful. Place them on an open gas burner, roast until the skin blackens, turning frequently, remove and place the peppers into a plastic bag to sweat. The skins will become loose and make peeling very easy.

GRILLED SHELLFISH ON A SKEWER WITH TOMATOES AND SWEET PEPPERS

SERVES 4

Ingredients

8 scallops
16 mussels, cooked, taken out of their shells
16 large clams, taken out of their shells
16 king prawns, cooked and peeled
21 tbsps olive oil

Tomatoes and Sweet Peppers

1 (175g) red bell pepper, cored, seeded and diced
50ml olive oil
1 onion chopped finely
4 cloves garlic, crushed and chopped finely
pinch cayenne pepper
3 medium tomatoes, peeled, seeded and diced
pinch of saffron
1 tbsp fresh herbs, parsley and basil
125ml dry white wine
salt and freshly ground white pepper

Preparation

Take four skewers and thread the seafood alternately on them. Keep refrigerated.

In a heavy sauté pan, heat 50ml olive oil, sauté the onion, garlic and cayenne pepper together for 5 minutes. Stir in the tomatoes, peppers and saffron. Pour in the white wine and cook for 30 minutes over a medium heat until all the liquid is absorbed. Season and add the fresh herbs. Keep warm.

Place the skewer on a tray and put under a pre-heated grill until the scallops are cooked. Serve on top of the tomato and pepper mixture.

CHEF'S TIP

The skewers can also be breadcrumbed and fried in a deep fryer at 180 C (350 F) until golden brown. A white wine sauce goes with this dish very well (see page 130).

MEAT AND GAME

Britain has a wonderful supply of meat and game. The grazing land for cattle is excellent and therefore the quality of the meat is good. Beef, lamb and chicken seem the most popular meats but over the last few years I have definitely seen an increase in pork, venison and game birds being consumed.

Modern styles of cooking have brought a change towards lighter dishes and chefs seem to pay more attention to the length of the cooking process and are using more varied and exciting recipes. Mind you I still believe there is no substitute for a good traditional tasty stew.

When roasting poultry always place the largest part of the bird towards the back of the oven as ovens are generally hotter there so the bird will cook more evenly. Always salt and pepper meat immediately before and after cooking in a hot oven.

The sauces in some of these recipes can be used for other birds and meat, just try experimenting.

RECIPES

PAN-FRIED MEDALLIONS OF VENISON ON A BED OF CARAMELISED APPLES, SERVED WITH A BLACK PEPPER CIDER SAUCE

SERVES 4

This is my favourite venison dish. When served with an apple and potato gratin and sweet and sour leeks, it makes a wonderful main course for that special dinner party.

Ingredients

700g Venison loin cut into 8 x 90g medallions

Sweet and sour leeks (see page 82)

Potato and apple gratin (see page 92)

Caramelised apples
2 apples   50g unsalted butter
dash of lemon juice   icing sugar to taste,
                                       to caramelise the apples

Black pepper cider sauce
225ml veal stock or light chicken   125ml double cream
  stock   1 tbsp crushed black
1 tbsp unsalted butter   peppercorns to taste
125ml red wine   125ml cider (medium dry)
2 sprigs of thyme   2 cloves of garlic
4 shallots   50ml Calvados (optional)

Preparation

Sauté the medallions until rare – about 2 minutes on each side.

Caramelised apples
Peel and core the apples and cut them first in quarters, then each quarter into 4 segments. Melt the butter in a frying pan and fry the apple segments. Sieve the icing sugar over, add the lemon juice and slightly caramelise the apples. They should be

slightly crisp. Keep warm. The apples can be caramelised a few hours before.

Black pepper cider sauce
Sauté shallots and garlic add the thyme, red wine and cider and reduce by half. Add the stock and reduce by half again. Over a medium heat pour in the cream and the Calvados; reduce until the sauce begins to thicken, whisk in the butter. Sieve and keep warm and add the crushed peppercorns.

Presentation

Arrange 2 venison medallions on a bed of caramelised apples off centre on a plate, place the gratin at the top of the plate and arrange a quantity of sweet and sour leeks. Pour sauce around the venison medallions and serve.

GRILLED VENISON SAUSAGES ON AN ONION COMPOTE

SERVES 6

Ingredients

1 kg haunch of venison
half an onion
1 chilli (deseeded)
1 red pepper
4 cloves garlic
1 tbsp fresh thyme and chives
300g fresh lard
100ml brandy (optional)
100ml red wine
1 egg
225g brioche crumbs or breadcrumbs
salt and pepper
pig's caul for wrapping the sausages or sausage casings (see page 78)

Onion compote
500g small onions, peeled
50ml red wine vinegar
150ml good red wine
150ml water
2 tbsps honey
80g butter
Freshly ground black pepper

Preparation

Remove all the sinews from the venison and mince finely. Very finely chop the onion, pepper, garlic, thyme, chives and chillies. Combine the meat with the vegetables, herbs and lard and mince again to blend well. Add the brandy and wine, mixing well. Beat in the egg and add to the meat. Add sufficient breadcrumbs for the mixture to hold its shape. Season and rinse the sausage casings under the tap. Force the meat into the skins or ask your butcher, he might fill them for you.

Onion compote

Slice the onions very finely. In a saucepan sweat the onions with the vinegar and the red wine until the liquid is totally absorbed. Add the water and continue cooking over a low heat for 30 minutes. Stirring occasionally so the onion doesn't stick. Add the honey and the butter and mix well together, season with salt and pepper. Keep warm.

Grill the sausages on a barbecue or under a hot grill. Divide onion compote on a pre-heated dinner plate, place a sausage on top and serve with creamy mashed potatoes

ROAST PIGEON AND WILD MUSHROOMS IN A PASTRY CASE SERVED WITH A RED WINE SAUCE

SERVES 4

Ingredients

2 pigeons
wild mushrooms (use as many as you like)
2 tbsps oil

Red Wine Sauce (see page 78)

Puff pastry case
half packet (225g) of puff pastry
1 egg yolk

Preparation

Thaw the pastry as per instructions on the packet. Place them on a lightly floured worktop and cut into shape as required. Prepare egg wash with yolk and a little water, brush the pastry cases and mark slightly with a knife. Bake in a hot oven until golden brown, and cooked through. Set aside.

Seal the pigeon with the oil in a saucepan and cook in a hot oven for 11 minutes. Remove and leave to rest. Fry wild mushrooms, season with salt and pepper and keep warm.

Presentation

Slice the pigeon into portions. Cut the top of each pastry case and fill the lower half with mushrooms, followed by the sliced pigeon. Pour the sauce carefully on and around the pastry case and finish with a pastry top.

CHEF'S TIP

There is no real season for pigeons but they are at their best between May and October, because they have had a good summer living off the farmer's fields.

When baking pastry cases arrange two weights at the end of the baking tray with a cooling rack on top. Bake cases in the oven. The cases will hit the top of the rack and keep a good shape; remove the rack after 10 minutes and continue to cook the cases through so they are not soggy inside.

BREAST OF PHEASANT IN ALMONDS WITH SWEET AND SOUR LEEKS

SERVES 4

Ask your butcher for young hen birds, they are more tender.

Ingredients

4 pheasants (young hen birds)
2 eggs
50g plain flour
3 tbsps white breadcrumbs
100g flaked almonds
100g butter
3 tbsps oil
salt and freshly ground black pepper

Sauce

1 onion, peeled and chopped
60g butter
100ml red wine
200ml double cream

1 sprig of thyme
2 cloves of garlic, peeled
   and chopped

Preparation

Cut off four breasts from the birds. Season the breasts with salt and pepper, whisk the eggs with a little water, mix the breadcrumbs with the almonds. Coat the breasts in flour, dust off then dip them in the egg mixture and then the almond and breadcrumbs, press firmly on to the breasts and shape. In a heavy saucepan sweat the onion and garlic in butter till golden brown. Pour in the wine and reduce by three quarters, add the thyme and the double cream, reduce to the right consistency. Put through a sieve pressing the onion and garlic well, season.

Heat the oil in a frying pan and fry the breasts on both sides until they are brown. Place in a hot oven with the butter for 5–6 minutes. Remove from the oven and leave to rest for 5 minutes.

Pour the sauce on to pre-heated dinner plates, arrange the pheasant breasts, sliced at an angle on the sauce. Serve with sweet and sour leeks (see page 82).

ROAST PHEASANT WITH PINE NUTS, CRISPY BACON SERVED WITH A BRANDY CREAM SAUCE

SERVES 4

Christmas is the time to indulge yourself with lovely poultry, game, stuffings, tasty sauces and wonderful desserts. The smell of home-baked mince pies and Christmas puddings all add to the enjoyment. Here is a good Christmas recipe wich I think you will enjoy.

Ingredients

2 small pheasants
salt and freshly milled black pepper
2 tbsps oil
1 tbsp butter

Sauce
2 tbsps oil
1 small onion, peeled
1 stick of celery, diced
1 small carrot, diced
300ml chicken stock
2 sprigs of thyme
200ml double cream
salt and pepper
50ml brandy
50ml white wine

Garnishes
2 tbsps pine nuts
20g butter
4 slices of rindless bacon

Spiced Cranberry Relish (see page 138)

Preparation
Sauce

Heat the oil in a saucepan. Add the diced onion, carrot and celery and sauté until the vegetables are lightly brown, add the brandy and white wine and reduce by half. Add the chicken stock and thyme and season lightly with salt and simmer until stock is reduced by two thirds.

Strain juices through a fine sieve, add cream and reduce until sauce slightly covers the back of the spoon. Season with salt if necessary and freshly milled pepper. Keep warm.

Garnishes

Fry the pine nuts in 20g of butter until golden brown and drain them on a piece of kitchen paper. Fry the bacon in a frying pan until the slices are very crisp. Remove bacon and keep warm.

Roast Pheasant

Season pheasant and seal in hot oil on both sides, place in a pre-heated oven 200°C (400°F, Gas Mark 6) for 30–45 minutes. Remove from the oven and allow to rest before carving.

CHEFS TIP

A trick to make the carving easier is to remove the wishbone before cooking.

ROAST QUAIL STUFFED WITH WILD MUSHROOMS ON A BED OF BEETROOT SERVED WITH A MADEIRA SAUCE

SERVES 4

A confit of shallots is a wonderful accompaniment to this dish.

Ingredients

Stuffed Quail
8 boned quail

Stuffing
4 oz chicken breast, finely chopped
1 clove garlic, finely chopped
225g wild mushrooms, finely chopped
2 shallots, finely chopped
1 sprig of fresh thyme
pinch of Chinese 5 spice (optional)
splash of brandy

Beetroot (see page 84)

Shallot Confit
clarified butter   10 shallots
salt and pepper   sprig of thyme

Preparation

Sauté the shallots and garlic together, add the wild mushrooms and the splash of brandy, then the thyme and spices, leave to cool. Add the chicken breast and check seasoning, pass through a food processor until well mixed. Stuff the quail and roast in the oven for 10 minutes at 220°C (440°F, Gas Mark 7–8). Remove and leave to rest.

Shallot Confit
Place shallots in a foil parcel, cover with the butter, add the thyme, salt and pepper and bake in the oven until tender.

Sauce

When the quail are cooked remove to a resting tray, deglaze the pan with madeira and reduce by a half, add some veal stock and reduce to the right consistency, check seasoning and serve over and around the quail.

Presentation

Arrange two stuffed quail on a pre-heated dinner plate on top of the beetroot and arrange the shallots around. Pour the sauce over the quail and serve.

CHICKEN LEGS COOKED IN RED WINE, SERVED WITH CHIVE MASHED POTATO

SERVES 4

This is a good winter warmer and quite delicious. If you don't want to use chicken legs you can use poussin (baby chicken) or duck legs.

Ingredients

3 tbsps pure olive oil	4 chicken legs
salt and pepper	8 shallots
225g diced carrots	225g diced turnips
2 tbsps chopped thyme	3 crushed garlic cloves
225ml red wine	225g plum tomatoes (skinned and diced)
850ml chicken stock	115g crisp diced fried bacon

Preparation

Pre-heat the oven to 180°C (350°F, Gas Mark 4). Heat the oil in a large pan, season the chicken legs with salt and pepper and brown well, remove and place in a ovenproof casserole. To the pan add the onions, carrots, turnips, thyme and garlic, sauté until the vegetables begin to cook. Add the red wine, plum tomatoes and chicken stock and cook over a medium heat for 10 minutes. Pour the vegetable mixture over the chicken in the casserole and cook for one and a quarter hours. When the chicken is cooked add the chopped crispy bacon and serve with the chive mashed potatoes.

Chive mashed potatoes

When making the mashed potatos add one clove of peeled garlic with butter and a little milk, salt and pepper, beat well then add 2 tablespoons of chopped chives. Remember to remove the clove of garlic before serving.

CHICKEN WITH TOMATO SAUCE HOT PEPPER AND PANCETTA

SERVES 4

Because chicken is so neutral in flavour, I find it one of the best meats to use for Mediterranean dishes and Asian salads.

Ingredients

125ml plus 2 tbsps of olive oil
4 slices of pancetta (diced)
4 chicken breasts
2 medium onions
2 tsps of dried chillies (or to taste)
175ml white wine
425ml tomato sauce (see page 135)
basil (finely chopped)
finely chopped fresh parsley
salt and pepper

Preparation

Heat 2 tablespoons of olive oil in a small sauté pan over medium heat. Add the pancetta and cook until crispy for about 10 minutes. Remove the pancetta from the pan and reserve the fat.

Heat 125ml of oil in a large sauté pan over a high heat. Add the chicken breasts and cook until lightly browned on all sides (about 4 minutes). Remove the chicken and set aside. Return pancetta fat to the pan, add the onion and cook until tender, add the chilli to taste and stir in the pancetta and wine. Cook until liquid is reduced by half, stir in the tomato sauce and add the chicken breasts, simmer until the chicken is cooked, about 4 minutes. Add the parsley and basil, season to taste. Serve hot in the middle of a table in an earthenware pot.

CHEF'S TIP

Try this dish garnished with spinach tagliatelle and hot garlic bread. You can use passata instead of the tomato sauce.

MUSTARD ROAST TURKEY WITH MUSHROOM STUFFING AND CRANBERRY RELISH

SERVES 8

Turkeys are best eaten young from seven months up to one year old, after which they start to become tough and less suitable for roasting. It is preferable to choose a hen bird, even though you may have to pay a little more for it. Roasting is the most popular method of cooking but care is needed as the flesh of turkey is fine and delicate and can be dry if over-cooked. It is important to use plenty of fat when cooking in order to keep the flesh moist, baste the bird from time to time. It is also essential to allow the roast turkey to rest for at least 30 minutes before carving – this enables the flesh to firm up and stay moist.

Ingredients

4.5kg (10lb) oven-ready turkey
3 tbsps Dijon mustard
butter or olive oil
mushroom stuffing (see page 101)

Preparation

Spoon the stuffing into the neck end only and place any remaining stuffing in a greased oven proof dish. Secure the flap of skin over the neck end with a fine skewer or cocktail sticks. Dot the stuffing in the oven proof dish with butter and cover with foil.

Place the turkey on a large roasting tin. Spread the breast and legs thinly with the mustard. Dot the turkey generously with butter or oil and grind some black pepper.

Cook at 200°C (400°F, Gas Mark 6) for one hour and then turn the oven down for a further two hours. Put the excess stuffing in the oven to bake for about one hour. The turkey will be a rich golden brown when ready, but test the thickest part of the leg with a skewer to ensure that it is fully cooked. The juices will run clear if the bird is ready. Serve with bread sauce (see page 139).

MARINATED PAN-FRIED DUCK BREAST, KARL LÖRDERER

SERVES 4

This recipe was given to me by one of my mentors who helped me become a master chef, so I have named it after him.

Ingredients

4 duck breasts

Marinade
juice and zest of 1 orange
1 inch piece of ginger, grated finely
150ml dry sherry
6 shallots, chopped finely
1 tsp honey
1 tbsp olive oil
5 tbsps Soy sauce
300ml stock, chicken, duck etc
2 tbsps olive oil for frying the ducks

Preparation

Score the top of the duck breast. Make the marinade, mix all the above ingredients together except the chicken stock. Place the breasts in the marinade and refrigerate for at least 2 hours. Remove the breasts from the marinade, pat dry and pan-fry them in olive oil on both sides until they are brown, place in a hot oven, skin side down, for 5 minutes. Remove from the oven and leave to rest. Add the duck marinade to the chicken stock and reduce until the sauce reaches the right consistency, strain through a fine sieve into a pan, season with finely milled pepper, keep warm.

CHEF'S TIP

If you find it difficult to remove the zest from the grater use a pastry brush and brush down the grater on a slight angle. This seems to work well. The marinade described here can also be used for chicken or pigeon.

BAKED TENDERLOIN OF PORK IN FILLO PASTRY WITH STILTON CHEESE

SERVES 4

Why not try this simple but tasty British pork dish;
served with a delicious, creamy chive sauce.

Ingredients

2 tenderloins of pork
2 tbsps oil
8 large leaves of spinach
115g Stilton cheese

salt and pepper
12 sheets of fillo pastry
50g melted butter

Sauce

20g butter
2 small shallots finely chopped
40ml Vermouth
60ml red wine
300ml chicken stock

100ml double cream
salt and pepper
1 small bunch of chopped
  chives

Preparation

Trim the 2 pork tenderloins, cut each tenderloin into 4 pieces. Flatten slightly with a mallet. Heat the oil in a frying pan and seal the medallions on both sides. Allow to cool and pat dry. Bring a large pot of water to the boil add salt and plunge in the washed spinach leaves for a few seconds. Transfer to iced water, drain and pat dry.

Place one prepared medallion on each spinach leaf, divide the Stilton into 4 pieces and place them on the medallions. Place the second medallion on top and fold the spinach over to make small parcels. Sprinkle with salt and pepper. Leave in the refrigerator for 30 min.

Unfold the fillo pastry and place 4 sheets next to each other, brush each sheet with melted butter and place another sheet on top of each 4 sheets and repeat the process twice. Place the tenderloin parcel at one end and fold over fillo pastry, leaving ends open, brush with butter. Place parcels on a buttered tray and bake in a pre-heated oven at 180°C (350°F, Gas Mark 4) for 8–10 min.

Sauce
Sweat the finely diced shallots in the butter, add the Vermouth, red wine and the stock and reduce by two-thirds. Add the double cream and reduce until sauce becomes creamy. Season, keep warm. Add the chopped chives to the sauce.

Presentation

Cut the baked tenderloin parcels three times at a slight angle and place on pre-heated dinner plates. Pour around sauce and serve immediately.

ROAST LOIN OF LAMB WITH HERBS AND A BREADCRUMB COATING

SERVES 4

Ingredients

1 loin of lamb
olive oil
1 tbsp Dijon mustard

Garlic and Rosemary Sauce

6 cloves garlic
200ml white wine
200ml water
200ml lamb stock
salt and pepper
1 tbsp rosemary

Herb and Breadcrumb Coating

115g breadcrumbs
1 tsp each of chopped chervil, tarragon, parsley, basil, chives

salt and pepper
1 small onion (chopped fine)

Preparation

Preheat the oven to 220°C (425°F, Gas Mark 7). Make the sauce by leaving the skins on the garlic, and gently bring them to the boil in a mixture of white wine, water and lamb stock. Cook until tender. Pass the garlic mixture through a sieve, pressing well. Reduce by half, adjust seasoning and consistency to taste.

Put the chopped onion in a small pan with some water, boil the onion until soft, remove from the water and drain in a sieve and allow to cool. Add the breadcrumbs, mix well then add the herbs and season with salt and freshly ground pepper.

Seal the lamb in hot oil in a skillet pan and then transfer to a baking tray. Mix the breadcrumbs, herbs and seasoning. Coat the outer surface of the lamb with a thin layer of Dijon mustard and then cover with the breadcrumb mixture, pressing down well to bind the crumbs. Return the lamb to the baking tray and place in the oven and cook for 10 minutes. Remove from the oven and leave to rest.

Carve the meat into portions and place on plates with the vegetables of your choice, pouring the sauce over and around the meat before serving.

FRESH CHICKEN LIVERS WITH GRAPES ON AN APPLE POTATO GRATIN

SERVES 4

*Chicken livers are seldom used these days but when served,
as in the following recipe they are delicious.*

Ingredients

450g chicken livers (fresh or frozen)
200g seedless grapes (halved)
4 portions of potato and apple gratin (see page 92)
60ml port
100ml brown veal stock (see page 149)
75g butter
50ml double cream

Preparation

Warm 4 portions of apple potato gratin in a pre-heated oven.

Heat 30g of the butter in a frying pan and fry the livers until they are golden brown but still pinkish on the inside. Transfer to a tray lined with kitchen paper. Add port and veal stock to the pan juices and reduce until it slightly starts to thicken, strain through a sieve, bring to the boil again and reduce the heat and whisk in the double cream, adjust the seasoning. Add the grapes and carefully warm in the sauce.

Place the apple potato gratin on pre-heated dinner plates. Divide the chicken livers equally on top and cover with the hot sauce.

OVEN ROASTED FILLET OF BEEF FILLED WITH MUSHROOMS AND HERBS

SERVES 4

This is an elegant main course for a special dinner, serve with creamed mashed potatoes and sautéed cherry tomatoes.

Ingredients

4 x 175g portions of fillet steak

Red wine Sauce
3 shallots, finely chopped
225ml red wine
225ml veal stock or beef stock
2 fresh plum tomatoes, peeled, seeded and finely chopped
freshly ground black pepper to taste
25g chopped olives (optional)

Filling
115g mushrooms, diced
1 clove garlic
4 shallots finely chopped
25g ham, chopped
1 tbsp sherry or brandy
1 tbsp fresh thyme leaves or 1 tsp crushed dried thyme
1 tbsp olive oil
1 tbsp tarragon leaves

Preparation

Pre-heat oven to 220°C (425°F, Gas Mark 7).

Sauté mushrooms, shallots, garlic; add the sherry and flame for 30 seconds. Then add the ham, pepper thyme and tarragon; sauté for 5 minutes; allow to cool. Cut the fillet steak three-quarters the way through, distribute the mushroom filling between the 4 steaks. The steaks can then be wrapped in pig's caul or a piece of cheesecloth and tied to hold in the filling, if using pig's caul sauté in a pan on both sides for 1 minute then cook in the oven for 5 minutes for medium rare. Remove from the oven and leave to rest.

To prepare the sauce, sauté the shallots in the same pan in which the steaks were cooked, add the remaining ingredients and reduce until the right consistency is reached.

Place the steaks on a potato recipe of your choice, pour the sauce over and around the steaks and garnish.

VEGETABLES AND ACCOMPANIMENTS

For many of the main courses in this book I have suggested recipes I think are good accompaniments. The recipes for almost all the garnishes are in this chapter of vegetables.

Vegetables are one of the most neglected foods, which is a great pity because they can make a big impact on your main dish if prepared with a little love and care. Why are the Chinese considered to be one of the world's best vegetable cooks? It is because they care. They respect the colour, flavour, and texture of the vegetables. They also know how to combine them with fish, meat and game so well.

I like to use young vegetables, they are sweet and most tender and need very little cooking, but whatever the vegetable buy the freshest available and ones which will add a little colour to the meal.

RECIPES

SWEET AND SOUR LEEKS
SERVES 4

This is a wonderful way of preparing leeks and one of my favourite recipes.
It goes well with chicken, pork or fish.

Ingredients

1kg leeks
2 cloves of garlic
1 tbsp sugar
4 tbsps olive oil
juice of 1 lemon
1 tbsp Soy sauce (optional)

Preparation

Clean the leeks thoroughly. Cut off the tough green part. Cut the leeks into longish slices.

Fry the crushed garlic and sugar in hot oil until the sugar caramelise slightly.

Add the leeks and turn them a little over moderate heat. Sprinkle with lemon juice. Cover and stew gently over a low heat until tender.

Serve hot or cold.

DEEP-FRIED CAULIFLOWER WITH GARLIC AND PAPRIKA OIL

SERVES 4

Ingredients

450g cauliflower florets
2 tbsps olive oil
2 garlic cloves – crushed
2 tbsps white wine vinegar
1 tbsp paprika
3 tbsps hot water
sunflower oil for deep-frying
seasoning

Batter
75g plain flour
5 tsps cornflour
pinch of salt
2 tsps baking powder
175ml water

Preparation

To make the batter, mix all the ingredients together in a bowl until smooth. Cover and chill until needed.

Bring a pan of water to the boil and cook the cauliflower for 5-6 minutes until almost tender, drain and leave to cool.

To make garlic and paprika oil, heat the olive oil in a frying pan over a medium heat. Add the garlic and cook gently for 1 minute to flavour the oil, then remove with a slotted spoon. Pour vinegar into the oil and add paprika and water and cook, stirring continuously for 1 minute. Set aside.

Heat the sunflower oil in a small, heavy-based pan. Dip the cauliflower into the batter and deep-fry for 2-3 minutes.

Remove with a slotted spoon and drain on kitchen paper. Transfer to a serving dish and pour the oil over to serve

BEETROOT WITH HONEY AND GINGER

SERVES 4

Ingredients

750g fresh beetroot
15g butter
2.5cm (1 inch) ginger, grated
2 tbsps clear honey
1 tbsp lemon juice
seasoning

Preparation

Wash and peel the beetroot and cut into 7.5cm (3 inch) strips. Melt the butter in a saucepan and add beetroot and grated ginger. Cook over a gentle heat for 4–5 minutes, stirring frequently.

Add honey and 120ml water, season, cover and cook over a low heat for 25 minutes. Add lemon juice and serve hot.

STIR-FRIED VEGETABLES

*The oyster sauce and Soy give the vegetables
an authentic lightly-glazed Chinese flavour.*

Ingredients

1 tbsp peanut oil
225g mangetout peas
115g oyster mushrooms
115g English mushrooms
115g red pepper strips
115g yellow pepper strips
half an aubergine cut into slices
half a medium bok choy (Chinese cabbage)
  cut into 1 inch chunks (or use Savoy cabbage)
6 broccoli florets
150ml of chicken stock (heated)
1 tbsp of Soy sauce
salt
freshly ground pepper
2 tbsps oyster sauce

Preparation

Heat the oil in a wok or a large skillet over high heat. Stir fry
all of the vegetables coating them with the oil. Pour in the
stock, oyster sauce and Soy sauce and stir until the vegetables
are *al dente*. Season with salt and pepper to taste keeping in
mind that the Soy sauce is already salty. Serve immediately.

CHEF'S TIP

*Oyster sauce is an
excellent all-purpose
seasoning for pasta, meat
and seafood and it
will keep indefinitely
in a refrigerator.*

STIR-FRIED SWEET AND SOUR SAVOY CABBAGE

SERVES 4

Ingredients

half a Savoy cabbage
8 shiitake mushrooms (or English)
2 tbsps olive oil
2 tbsps granulated sugar
2 tbsps red wine vinegar
2 tbsps Soy sauce
salt and pepper to taste

Preparation

Heat the oil in a large skillet and add the mushrooms and cook briefly until tender. Add the cabbage and stir-fry, shaking the pan and tossing the cabbage with a slotted spoon. Add the sugar, vinegar and Soy sauce, cook for 3 minutes more. Remove from the heat before the cabbage loses its crispness and colour.

Serve with grilled fish or meaty dishes.

CURRIED VEGETABLE FRITTERS

SERVES 4–6

Ingredients

1 large potato, peeled and cut in half-inch dice
1 large onion, peeled and diced
2 carrots, peeled and diced
3 stalks celery, diced
2 courgettes diced
3 tbsps olive oil
1 tbsp garlic, chopped
2 tbsps curry powder
1 tbsp passata

Fritter Batter
225g flour
125ml water
50ml milk
half tsp baking powder
half tsp salt

Preparation

Sauté the diced vegetables in olive oil until the vegetables are browned on all sides and cooked through. Add the garlic to mix and cook for 1 minute more before adding the curry powder, then add the tomato passata. Cook for 2 minutes more then remove from the heat and allow to cool in a clean bowl.

Combine the batter ingredients, then let rest for 20 minutes in the refrigerator. Deep fry the vegetables. Using a large tablespoon, spoon portions of the vegetables and batter into the fryer until golden brown.

Cook at 160°C (320°F) in the fryer.

ASPARAGUS MOUSSE
SERVES 4

This is a good way to use up the end cuts of asparagus.

Ingredients

250g end cuts of asparagus   50g double cream
1 shallot, finely chopped   salt to taste
40g butter   freshly milled pepper
1 egg   pinch of salt
3 egg yolks

Preparation

Sweat the finely chopped shallots in the butter, add the asparagus and cook for a few minutes. Allow to cool. Transfer with the egg, egg yolks, cream and seasoning to a liquidizer. Blend well. Strain through a fine sieve and fill generously buttered moulds. Poach in a water bath in a moderate oven 180°C (350°F, Gas Mark 4) for 15 minutes.

Serve with fish or white meat dishes.

POTATO CROQUETTES
MAKES 24 CROQUETTES

These croquettes can be prepared in advance and refrigerated or frozen.

Ingredients

4 large baking potatoes
2 large eggs, lightly beaten
half tsp nutmeg
115g Parmesan cheese
salt and pepper to taste
1 tbsp chopped fresh thyme and sage
115g pine nuts
225g toasted breadcrumbs
vegetable oil for frying

Preparation

Bake potatoes until tender, about 1 hour in a pre-heated oven at 230°C (450°F, Gas Mark 8). Let cool enough to handle. Cut the potatoes in half and scoop out the pulp. mash lightly. Combine all of the ingredients except the breadcrumbs and oil.

Shape into 4cm (1.5-inch) logs and roll in the breadcrumbs to coat. Fry at temperature 180°C (350°F) until golden brown.

This recipe is very good served with roast turkey or grilled fish.

MASHED POTATO
SERVES 5-6

I love mashed potatoes, they remind me of when I was a little boy.
My mother would grate cheddar cheese on them – delicious!

Ingredients

1.2kg (2.5Ibs) baking potatoes, peeled and cut into large chunks
salt
175g butter, diced
freshly ground white pepper
2 cloves garlic peeled – left whole
175ml milk

Preparation

Cover the potatoes with lightly salted water and cook in a saucepan until tender. Drain well.

Mash the potatoes in a large saucepan, return to the stove and put on a low heat and beat in the butter, milk and garlic cloves until light and creamy. Pass through a course sieve to remove lumps and garlic. Serve mashed potatoes with anything you like.

CHEF'S TIP

Try stirring in some crispy fried onions or leeks for a tasty alternative.

FRENCH FRIES

Preparation

Add sliced potatoes to the fryer at 120°C (250°F) for 3–4 minutes. Remove and place on paper towels to drain. The blanched potatoes can now be cooled and refrigerated for as long as a couple of days. When ready to use, turn up the fryer to 180°C (360°F) degrees and cook until golden and crisp.

CHEF'S TIP

The key to avoiding soggy french fries is to fry them twice.

POTATO AND APPLE GRATIN

This recipe compliments both duck and venison.

Ingredients

150g green apples
100g onions
1 clove of garlic, peeled
200 ml cream

300g potatoes
130g butter
salt and pepper
80g grated tasty cheese

Preparation

Peel the apples and grate them into a bowl, peel the potatoes and cut them in thin slices, peel and slice the onions and sweat them together with the apples in 100g butter. Allow to cool and mix them with the sliced potatoes.

Chop the garlic and add it together with the salt and pepper. Butter a gratin dish, put in the mixture and pour the cream equally over the mix and sprinkle with cheese. Pre-heat the oven to 180°C (350°F, Gas Mark 4), place the dish in the oven on the bottom shelf for approximately 1 hour.

When cold use a pastry cutter to cut out the portions you require. Re-heat in the oven. The potato gratin will keep for 5 days covered in the fridge.

TOMATO AND COURGETTE GRATIN

SERVES 6–8

Ingredients

1.5kg (3 lbs) plum tomatoes (or good ripe English)
1.5kg (3lbs) courgettes
115g breadcrumbs
115g Parmesan freshly grated (or tasty Cheddar)
chopped parsley and thyme
seasoning
125ml olive oil

Preparation

Pre-heat the oven to 190°C (375°F, Gas Mark 5). Slice the tomatoes and courgettes into quarter-inch thick round slices as uniformly as possible. In an oven-proof gratin dish overlap the tomatoes and courgettes, sprinkle with olive oil and bake until golden and crusty, about 30 minutes. Sprinkle with the breadcrumbs and Parmesan cheese. Bake until golden and crusty, about 30 minutes. Sprinkle with chopped parsley, thyme or basil as preferred.

CHERRY TOMATOES WITH MANGETOUT AND SHALLOTS

SERVES 4

Ingredients

2 tbsps olive oil
3 shallots, finely diced
100g mangetout, cut into strips
350g cherry tomatoes, halved
2 tbsps chopped parsley
seasoning

Preparation

Heat the oil and cook shallots in a frying pan for 3-4 minutes until tender. Add mangetout and cook for 2 minutes. Stir in the tomatoes and cook until soft. Add parsley, season and serve.

BAKED RED PEPPERS WITH GARLIC AND TOMATOES

SERVES 4

Ingredients

2 garlic cloves, thinly sliced
2 small tomatoes, halved
2 small red peppers, deseeded and halved
4 tsps olive oil
seasoning
2 tbsps chopped fresh parsley

Preparation

Place slices of garlic and half a tomato into each pepper half, drizzle a teaspoon of oil over each and season. Bake for 25–30 minutes until the pepper is tender. Sprinkle with parsley to serve.

BRAISED RED CABBAGE
SERVES 6

Ingredients

1 head of red cabbage
2 tbsps vinegar
1 medium onion peeled and finely sliced
225ml red wine
2 Golden Delicious apples, grated
2 tbsps redcurrant jelly
salt and freshly ground pepper
125g olive oil

Preparation

Remove and discard any outer damaged leaves, cut into quarters, cut away the hard cores, thinly slice the cabbage.

Put olive oil in a large pan, heat and add cabbage and stir for 10 minutes until all the cabbage is cooked, add the grated apple, sliced onions and redcurrant jelly, cook for 10 minutes more. Add the red wine, reduce the heat and slowly cook for 45 minutes, stirring occasionally. The liquid should have evaporated. Serve hot.

At the Horn of Plenty we serve this cabbage with game bird and venison.

CHEF'S TIP

The addition of chestnuts gives the cabbage a Christmas flavour. Keep checking the cabbage while cooking as it does tend to burn if not stirred.

SPINACH PASTA

SERVES 2

Ingredients

225g fresh spinach torn into smaller pieces
1 large egg
280g – 350g plain flour
pinch of salt

Preparation

Purée the spinach and egg in a food processor or blender. Add salt.
Add as much flour as you need to make a stiff dough, as the spinach
will continue to give off moisture while the dough rests.

CHEF'S TIP

I like to use uncooked spinach as I find this makes a lovely green pasta.

97

PASTA

Ingredients

175g plain flour
pinch of salt
1 large egg
2 tsps of water (or more if required)

Preparation

Mix the flour and salt on a work surface and shape it into a mound.
Make a well in the centre and drop in the egg and water. Stir the egg
in water together gradually, mixing in the flour from the side of the
well. Knead the dough with your hands until very smooth.

TEMPURA BATTER

Ingredients

85g plain flour
1.5 tbsps cornflour
1.5 tsps salt
2 tsps baking powder
175ml water

Preparation

To make the batter simply mix all of the ingredients together and stir
briefly – avoid stirring too much.

SRI LANKAN PASTRY

Ingredients

225g plain flour
2 tbsps of thick coconut-milk (optional)
115g clarified butter
1 egg
cold water
half tsp milk
salt

Preparation

Pour the flour into the mixing bowl and add the salt, coconut-milk, milk, butter and egg. Mix thoroughly with the fingers until smooth adding just enough cold water to make a very firm dough. Knead lightly and then chill.

CHEF'S TIP

To clarify butter put it into a saucepan and heat gently. Remove the pan from the heat and allow the residue to settle to the bottom of the pan. There will be a layer of milk solids on the bottom and a layer of foam on the top. Skim off and discard the layer of foam and slowly strain the melted butter, discarding the milk solids. The clarified butter can now be heated to a high temperatiure without burning. When clarified, butter has a fine, grainy texture and can heighten the flavours of many recipes. You can use clarified butter whenever butter is called for in a recipe.

Clarified butter will keep for 1 month in the refrigerator in a sealed container.

MUSHROOM STUFFING

Ingredients

1 chicken breast
1 onion – chopped
8 strips of bacon – chopped
1 tsp each of chopped tarragon, parsley and thyme
3 cloves garlic – chopped
450g mushrooms
225g bread crumbs
salt and pepper
1 egg – lightly beaten
1 apple, peeled , diced and sautéed

Mince the chicken breast and place in a bowl in the fridge. Lightly sauté the chopped onion, garlic, bacon and apple together until soft then add the chopped mushrooms. Cook for a further 2 minutes and place on a tray to cool.

When the mixture is cool add it to the chicken breast and mix well. Add the breadcrumbs, egg and fresh herbs. Finally add salt and pepper and place in a covered container in the refrigerator until ready to use.

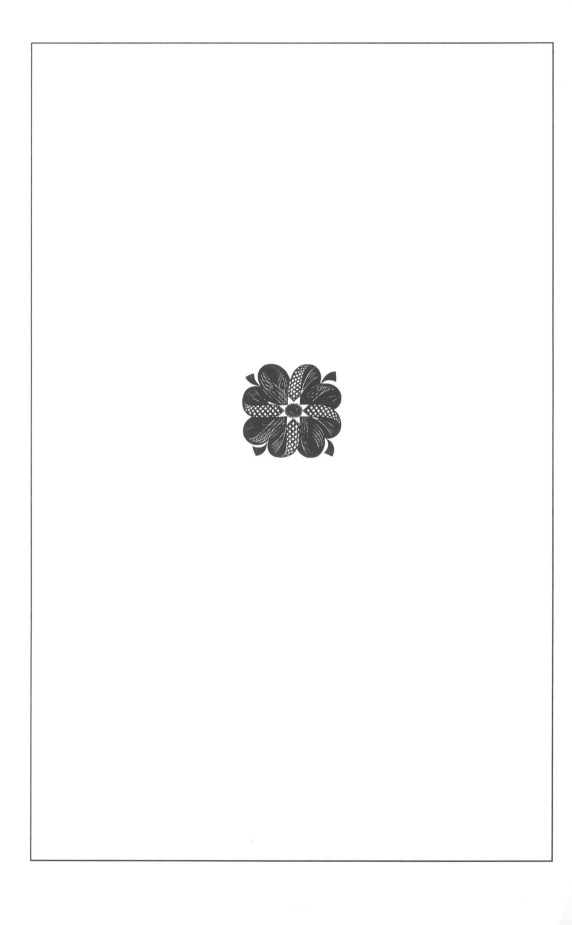

DESSERTS

Desserts occupy an important position on any menu because it will be your guests' last impression of the meal.

The desserts in this book range from the simplicity of a quick-and-easy lemon crème brûlée to an elegant passion fruit bavarois, through to the pure indulgence of a steamed chocolate and cardamom pudding with lashings of clotted cream.

I imagine most of you will be able to prepare these dessert recipes with ease. They will look good and should taste wonderful if you remember to buy the best ingredients and follow the recipes carefully.

RECIPES

POACHED PEARS, WRAPPED IN FILLO PASTRY, AND SERVED WITH A CARAMEL SAUCE

SERVES 4

Ingredients
4 small pears

Poaching liquid
725ml water
225ml dry white wine
115g granulated sugar
2 whole cloves
1 cinnamon stick

Pastry
450g package of fillo pastry – defrosted in the refrigerator
  overnight
225ml melted unsalted butter

Amaretto filling
(Mix all the ingredients below to form a firm paste)
125g Amaretto biscuits
125 ground almonds
4 tsps sugar
4 tsps butter

Caramel sauce
250ml double cream (and a little extra cream to thin the sauce)
250g sugar
150ml water

Preparation

Combine the poaching ingredients together. Bring to the boil and simmer for 10 minutes. Remove from the heat and add the pears, return to the boil and then simmer for 10 minutes. Remove the pears from the liquid so they do not continue to cook. When they have cooled completely, core the pears from the bottom, fill them with the Amaretto stuffing, dry any excess liquid from the pears.

CHEF'S TIP

The pears can be prepared up to three days in advance. When adding the cream to the caramel be very careful as the mixture tends to splatter.

Pre-heat the oven to 200°C (400°F, Gas Mark 6), to prepare the pastry allow 3 sheets of fillo pastry per pear. Brush each sheet with melted butter, layering them on top of the next sheet, place 1 pear in the centre of each pastry square, pull the four corners up towards the top and pinch around the stem leaving as much stem exposed as possible. Bake the pears until golden brown. While the pears are baking make the caramel sauce. Bring the water and sugar to the boil and boil until a nice golden brown remove from heat. In another pan bring the cream to the boil and add this a little at a time to the caramel, whisk carefully and return to the heat until all the caramel has dissolved.

Presentation

Place pears in the centre of 4 plates and pour over the caramel sauce and serve with an ice-cream of your choice.

PASSION FRUIT BAVAROIS WITH DICED EXOTIC FRUIT SERVED WITH A RASPBERRY COULIS

SERVES 8

CHEF'S TIP

If the creme Anglaise overcooks and curdles add a few drops of water or spirit and whisk to return the custard to a smooth texture. If all fails place in a liquidizer and whisk till smooth.

Ingredients

Creme Anglaise
300ml milk
4 egg yolks

1 vanilla pod
85g vanilla sugar

Fruit mixture
300ml passion fruit juice
1 tbsp sugar

50ml white wine
4 leaves of gelatine

Creme chantilly
300ml double cream

1 tbsp icing sugar

Diced Fruit
half a ripe mango
4 strawberries
raspberry coulis

1 kiwi fruit
1 passion fruit

Preparation

Creme Anglaise
Whisk the yolks and sugar, until thick and creamy. Put the milk and vanilla in a pan and bring to the boil. Pour on to the egg yolks mixture. Return to the saucepan and cook until the mixture thickens and coats the back of a spoon. Pass the custard through a fine sieve and cool immediately in a bowl resting on crushed ice.

Presentation

Tip out bavarois onto the centre of the plates, arrange fruits around the bavarois and dribble a little raspberry coulis over fruits. Place half of the passion fruit seeds on the top of each bavarois. Reduce by half the passion fruit juice, white wine and sugar, then strain. Dissolve 2 leaves of gelatine in a little water, whip the cream and 1 tablespoon of icing sugar to a soft ribbon. Mix gelatine into the creme anglaise and add the passion fruit mixture, stir well and fold in creme chantilly. Set in metal moulds.

LEMON CRÈME BRÛLÉE

SERVES 8 PEOPLE

Ingredients

6 egg yolks
280g sugar
4 eggs
juice of 6 lemons
juice of 2 oranges
300ml cream
225g light brown sugar

Preparation

Whisk yolks and sugar until smooth and white. Add eggs, lemon
juice and orange juice. Boil cream and whisk into the egg mixture.
pour into the ramekins and bake in a bain-marie with hot water for
about 30 minutes at 180°C (350°F Gas Mark 4).

When cooked, place in a bain-marie of iced water and cool.

Presentation

Turn out the crème brûlées on to a dessert plate and garnish with
fresh raspberries and chopped mint.

CARAMELISED APPLE AND ORIENTAL ORANGES SERVED IN A PANCAKE

SERVES 4–6

This recipe is quite wonderful, you can use the oriental oranges cold for garnishing other desserts or instead of a pancake you can make and fill a warm puff pastry basket .

Ingredients

Filling
125g plain flour
55g castor sugar
1 tbsp vanilla sugar
pinch of fine salt
3 eggs
300ml milk
butter

Apples
4–6 eating apples
sugar
water

Oriental Oranges
6 large oranges
100g sugar

1.5 tbsps Grand Marnier
1.5 tbsps of Grenadine syrup

Preparation

Mix the ingredients to make the pancake batter and leave to rest for 20 minutes. Segment the oranges, julienne the zest of 3 oranges, and save as much juice as possible. Blanch the zest 3 times in water.

Caramelise the sugar, add orange juice and cook to a light syrup. Add the Grenadine, Grand Marnier and zest. When cool, add orange segments and set aside.

Peel, core and cube the apples. Caramelise the sugar and water in a pan, add the apples and cook until tender. Then add the oriental oranges.

Presentation

Fill the pancakes with the apple and orange mixture. Fold over the pancake and serve with vanilla ice-cream or a sauce of your choice, caramel goes very well.

CHEF'S TIP

Raspberries or blackberries are also very delicious, sautéed with the apple. This dish can be made up a good few hours in advance and warmed in the oven with a little icing sugar sprinkled over the top. If you remove the top, bottom and labels from 4 small, clean, empty cans (i.e. baked bean tins) you can place the cans on a baking tray and fill them with the apple mixture, placing a pastry lid on top of each.

BLANCMANGE OF NUTS
WITH FRESH BERRIES
SERVES 4

Blancmange is rarely made these days which is a great shame because when made well it is a very nice light dessert to serve after a good meal.

Ingredients

50g ground almonds – soaked overnight in 250ml milk
50g mixed nuts chopped
half tsp icing sugar
50g castor sugar
3 egg yolks
6g gelatine
20ml liqueur of your choice
250ml whipping cream lightly whipped
450g mixed fresh berries, raspberries, blackcurrant strawberries etc

Preparation

Strain the milk in which the nuts have been soaking into a cheese cloth, firmly pressing on the ground almonds to get out all the liquid. Discard the nuts.

Dust the mixed nuts with icing sugar and caramelise them under the grill.

Mix together in a pan, castor sugar, egg yolks and half of the milk. Bring the other half to the boil, stir in the sugar and the egg mixture. Dissolve the gelatine in the liqueur and add to the milk mixture. Cook gently until the mixture coats the back of a spoon, be careful not to boil it. Pass through a fine sieve into a basin and allow to cool, stir from time to time to release any excess heat. Add the prepared nuts and when the mixture starts to thicken fold in the whipped cream. Place blancmange into lightly oiled moulds, cover and allow to set in a refrigerator.

Presentation

Plunge the moulds quickly into luke-warm water, and turn them out on to dessert plates. Arrange mixed berries around the blancmange and serve with any kind of fresh fruit sauce.

CHRISTMAS APPLE PIE
SERVES 8–10

This is my favourite apple pie, served hot or cold
with heaps of clotted cream, delicious!

Ingredients

450g sweet pastry
85g unsalted butter
2 tbsps of Calvados
2 tbsps of double cream
40g chopped dried apricots
1 tbsp of lemon juice
1 tsp of lemon zest
half tsp freshly grated nutmeg
1.5 tbsps of crystallised sugar

10 large Granny Smith apples
sugar
1 tbsp brandy
55g chopped dried prunes
25g chopped dried figs
2 tsps of ground cinnamon
1 tsp orange zest
1 egg white

Preparation

Prepare the Pastry
Divide the pastry into two parts, one a little larger then the other. On a lightly floured surface roll the smaller piece into a round approximately .5cm (quarter-inch) thick, large enough to overlap a 25cm x 5cm (10 x 2 inch) pie tin. Tuck the overhang back under, making a slightly thicker edging.

The Filling
Peel, core, and quarter the apples. Cut into .5cm (quarter-inch) slices. In a large frying pan melt the butter and brown until it has a slightly nutty aroma. Divide the apples and orange in the pan and coat with butter. Sprinkle in the sugar and over heat sauté the apples until lightly caramelised and tender, turn often so that the apples cook evenly. Pour in the Calvados and brandy and cook until the alcohol burns off. Pour in the cream and stir thoroughly. Transfer and spread over a large baking tray to cool. Pre-heat the oven to 200°C (400°F, Gas Mark 6).

Warm the remaining two tablespoons of Calvados. Combine the chopped prunes, apricots and figs in a bowl and pour the Calvados over, allow to infuse.

In a large bowl combine the cooled apples and fruit mixture. Stir in the lemon juice, cinnamon, lemon and orange zest and nutmeg.

Spoon the filling into the prepared pie tin, arrange the pastry disc on the top, brush the pastry with egg white and sprinkle with crystallised sugar. Bake for 30 minutes and then turn the oven down to 150°C (300°F, Gas Mark 2) and bake for a further 20 minutes. Cool on a rack.

Presentation

Serve with a brandy sauce or cinnamon ice cream

FRESH STRAWBERRIES TOPPED WITH A LIGHT WHITE CHOCOLATE MOUSSE

SERVES 4

July is the month for strawberries and the things you can make with them are endless. Strawberries need not only be eaten as a dessert they have a natural affinity with salmon and various salads, they contain only 26 calories per 100g and are a good source of vitamin C.

Ingredients

175g white chocolate
225ml double cream
1 egg yolk
1 whole egg

1–2 leaves of gelatine
1 lemon zest and juice
1 large punnet of local strawberries
4 brandy snap biscuits

Preparation

Place the eggs in a heat-proof bowl with the lemon zest and 1 tablespoon of juice. Beat over gently simmering water until the mixture is thick. Warm the gelatine with one tablespoon of lemon juice in a pan, if needed add 1 tablespoon of water. Fold in the melted chocolate and the gelatine into the sabayon mixture, then fold in the double cream bit by bit, refrigerate the mousse for 2 hours. Quarter strawberries and put them into individual dessert glasses, pipe chocolate mousse on top and serve with a brandy snap biscuit.

The mousse will keep fresh for a week in the refrigerator.

CHEF'S TIP

Check the base of the starwberry punnet to see if it is stained, if it is then it is a good indication that the bottom layer has been squashed. Fruit picked in the rain or left on display in wet weather will turn mouldy quickly.

BAKED WHITE CHOCOLATE CHEESECAKE

SERVES 8–10

Ingredients

225g sweet pastry (see page 125)

Caramelised pears
2 medium pears, peeled, cored
  and quartered
55g unsalted butter
85g sugar

Cream cheese mixture
175g sugar
4 eggs
1 tsp vanilla essence
225g white chocolate
650g cream cheese

CHEF'S TIP

When the cake has finished baking loosen it from the tin by running a knife around the edge, cool for 30 minutes at room temperature, cut the cheesecake with a hot knife, both these steps prevent cracking on the top.

Preparation

Preheat oven to 180°C (350°F, Gas Mark 4). Pour water halfway up the sides of a baking dish into which you can set a 20cm or 25cm (8-inch or 10-inch) spring-form tin. Let the water in the tin simmer.

On a lightly floured surface roll out the pastry on a baking sheet and bake until golden brown. Place in the cake tin. Set aside.

To caramelise the pears, sauté pears with the butter and sugar until lightly caramelised, spread evenly over the baked pastry.

Place the cream cheese in a mixer and add the sugar, mix well, add the eggs one at a time, add the vanilla and the melted white chocolate. Pour into the spring-form tin on the top of the pears. Wrap foil tightly around the outside of the tin and bake in a bain-marie for 55 to 60 minutes. Serve with strawberry or raspberry sauce.

DARK CHOCOLATE PARFAIT WITH A TANGERINE SAUCE

MAKES 1 TERRINE – SERVES 12

Many people find chocolate irresistible. Theobroma *'food of the gods', which is the botanical name, describes it well. Store chocolates well-wrapped in a cool place, dark chocolate will keep for years, milk and white chocolate because of the milk in them can become rancid in six to nine months.*

Ingredients

425ml cream
4 eggs
2 tbsps of Grand Marnier (optional)

450g dark chocolate
140g castor sugar

Tangerine sauce – serves 4

3 tangerines
30g castor sugar
pinch of allspice
2 tangerines into segments,
  to garnish

quarter tsp cornflour
pinch of ground cinnamon
pinch of cloves
a few sprigs of mint

Preparation

Melt chocolate, whisk eggs and sugar until thick and creamy then gently fold in the chocolate a little at a time, fold in half of the whipped cream and gently fold in the rest, adding brandy if desired. Pour into a lined terrine or mould and freeze until set.

Tangerine sauce
Peel tangerines, cut into quarters, discard the pips and blend the fruit with a tablespoon of water in a liquidizer. Strain through a sieve to remove all the stringy parts. Divide the liquid in half and place one part in a bowl and dissolve the cornflour in it. Place the other half in a shallow saucepan with the sugar and bring to the boil. Constantly stirring, add to the mixture with the dissolved cornflour. Bring to the boil. Reduce heat immediately. Stir until you have a smooth sauce and turn off the heat. Add spices. Turn out terrine mould by placing a hot towel around the mould, cut terrine into 2cm (three-quarters of an inch) slices and serve the sauce, tangerine segments and a sprig of mint.

CHEF'S TIP

If a few drops of water get into the chocolate as it melts it will stiffen. To soften it stir in vegetable oil, a teaspoonful at a time until it smoothes out.

STEAMED CHOCOLATE AND CARDAMOM PUDDING

SERVES 4

*This is a light, full flavoured pudding and
makes a wonderful winter dessert.*

Ingredients

3 egg yolks
50g unsalted butter
25g icing sugar
3 egg whites
25g castor sugar
50g flaked almonds
50g grated chocolate
pinch powdered cardamom
a few sprigs of mint
butter and extra castor sugar for coating the moulds

Preparation

Cream together the butter and icing sugar and add the egg yolks one
at a time. Beat well until the mixture is smooth. In a bowl whisk the
egg whites and castor sugar to form soft peaks, using a large spoon
fold in the almonds, grated chocolate, cardamom, the beaten egg
yolk and butter mixture.

Brush 4 flame-proof pudding moulds generously with butter and
sprinkle with castor sugar. Pour in the mixture and set pudding
moulds in a bain-marie (roasting tin) half filled with water. Bake in
a pre-heated oven at 160°C (325°F, Gas Mark 3) for 30 minutes.

Presentation

Turn out the hot puddings on to the centre of pre-heated flat dessert
plates. Pour ginger or orange sauce around the pudding. Garnish
with some orange segments and a small sprig of mint.

VANILLA DAIRY ICE CREAM

MAKES 1 LITRE

Ingredients

12 egg yolks
225g castor sugar
1 litre milk
1 vanilla pod
300ml double cream

Preparation

Whisk the yolks and sugar together. Put the milk, cream and scraped out vanilla seeds into a pan, bring to the boil, pour this over the egg yolks. Mix well. Return the mixture to a clean saucepan and cook for a few minutes, stirring continuously with a wooden spoon until the mixture thickens and coats the back of the spoon. Pass the mixture through a fine sieve and cool. Churn in an ice-cream maker.

CHEF'S TIP

If you do not have a ice-cream machine, put the mixture in a shallow freezing container and freeze until half frozen, turn the mixture out into a cold bowl, then beat until smooth, return to the freezer until firm.

BANANA AND HONEY
ICE CREAM
MAKES 1.7 LITRES (3 PINTS)

*This is one of my favourite ice creams and a good
way of using over-ripe bananas.*

Ingredients

600ml double cream
600ml milk
1 vanilla pod, split and scraped
3 large bananas, very ripe
6 egg yolks
6 tbsps castor sugar
2 tbsps honey
30ml rum

Preparation

In a large saucepan bring the cream and the milk to the boil with the
vanilla seeds. Remove from the heat and allow to infuse. Mash the
bananas well or purée in a food processor, set aside.

In a large bowl beat together the egg yolks and sugar until pale
yellow. Pour the cream mixture into the egg yolks whisking continuously. Return the mixture to the saucepan and cook over a low
heat until the mixture thickens enough to coat the back of a spoon.
Pour into a bowl and whisk, stir in the bananas, honey and rum.
Chill and churn in a ice-cream machine or use the same method
used for the vanilla ice-cream.

FRESH FRUIT SORBET

SERVES 4

Ingredients

225ml water
115g granulated sugar
225g puréed fruit – raspberries, strawberries, kiwis
  or a mixture of all

Preparation

Bring the water and sugar just to the boil, then lower the heat and simmer for 5 minutes. Remove from the heat and cool completely. When cold combine with the fruit purée. Churn in a ice-cream machine or place in a plastic container and freeze, then stir well every 15 minutes until frozen.

LEMON CURD

Ingredients

3 lemons – juice and zest
230g sugar
250g butter
4 whole eggs

Preparation

Mix all the above ingredients together. Whisk over a bain-marie (a large bowl sitting on a pan of water) until the mixture is thick and resembles lightly whipped cream. Set aside and leave to cool.

CHEF'S TIP

You can also turn this lemon curd mixture into a lovely light mousse for meringues by adding 300ml of lightly whipped cream, or serve it with fresh fruits.

CHOCOLATE PRALINE TRUFFLES

Ingredients

175g chocolate (milk or dark to your preference)
1 egg yolk
225ml of Irish cream liquer
ground praline to taste (see page 123)

To dip chocolates
225g bittersweet chocolate

Preparation

Cut the chocolate into 5cm (2-inch) pieces. In a heat-proof bowl melt the chocolate over gently simmering water. Do not let the water touch the bottom of the bowl. Turn off the heat and whisk in an egg yolk. Let stand over warm water until ready to use.

In a saucepan, scald the liquer and pour onto melted chocolate. Whisk together and then whisk in the praline.

Pour the mixture into a shallow tin in a layer 2.5cm (1-inch) thick and chill or freeze until set.

Form the truffles and dip in the chocolate. Place them on a tray in the refrigerator.

HAZELNUT CHOCOLATE SABLÉ COOKIES

Melt in the mouth Sablé cookies, this French version of shortbread has always been a favourite of mine.

Ingredients

55g hazelnuts
85g bittersweet chocolate (very cold)
115g icing sugar
140g unsalted butter
1 egg
quarter tbsp vanilla extract
225g flour
half tbsp of grated orange zest

Preparation

Pre-heat the oven to 160-170°C (325°F, Gas Mark 3). Spread hazelnuts on a baking sheet and toast for 8 to 10 minutes. Cool. Rub nuts in a clean tea towel to remove skins and set aside.

Chop chocolate by hand into pieces of approximately the size of rice.

In a food processor, process toasted hazelnuts with the icing sugar until they reach the same consistency as coarse corn meal. Set aside. Using the paddle attachment of an electric mixer, beat the butter and orange zest on medium speed until butter whitens and holds soft peaks. Add the flour and mix for a few seconds more. In a small bowl whisk together the eggs and vanilla and then beat into the batter mixture, finally beat in the hazelnut mixture and chopped chocolate until well combined.

Wrap the dough in clingfilm for at least 2 hours and refrig-erate.

Cook cookies at 150°C (300°F, Gas Mark 2) for 12 minutes or until lightly browned. Cool completely.

CHEF'S TIP

You can make the cookies for afternoon tea sandwiched together with some chocolate glaze.

FLORENTINES

Ingredients

85ml cream
60g honey   } boil to 110°C
60g butter
30ml glucose

175g mixed peel
100g nibbed almonds
115g flaked almonds
25g glacé cherries

Preparation

Boil the cream, honey, butter and glucose until the temperature reaches 110 degrees on the sugar meter.

Put the rest of the ingredients in the pan and stir for 20 seconds. Pour into a 12x18cm (7x5 inch) lined pastry tray and cook for approximately 20 minutes at 180°C (350°F, Gas Mark 4).

When cooked, cut into small squares.

PRALINE

Ingredients

115g flaked almonds
115g hazelnuts
225g sugar

Preparation

Roast nuts, remove the skins from the hazelnuts.

Cook the sugar until the caramel stage adding all the nuts. Stir
for 1 minute.

Pour on to an oiled tray and leave to cool. Break into pieces
and grind to a fine meal in a food processor. Store in an air-
tight jar.

CHEF'S TIP

*The praline will turn
into a paste if processed
too long.*

DARK CHOCOLATE GLAZE

The glaze is very versatile and is good for filling or coating a sponge cake.

Ingredients

225g dark chocolate
140g butter – unsalted
1 tbsp maple syrup (optional)
140g double cream
5 tbsps brandy

Preparation

Melt chocolate over a bain-marie.

Heat cream and brandy.

Whisk maple syrup into melted chocolate, gradually adding cream and brandy. Whisk the butter into the mixture until smooth.

Allow to cool for a few minutes, then pour over your cake or parfait or allow to cool and use for a filling.

To use again if mixture has gone too hard, re-heat in a heat-proof bowl over a pot of barely simmering water

SWEET PASTRY

MAKES 2 X 23CM (9 INCH) TART SHELLS

Always make pastry dough a few hours before using it, you will find it much easier to work with. Quantities can be increased and then portions can be divided for freezing.

Ingredients

250g plain flour
125g unsalted butter
1 tbsp milk or water
100g sugar
2 egg yolks
pinch of salt

Preparation

Sift flour into a bowl, add salt and sugar and the butter, cut into pieces. Work lightly and quickly until the mixture becomes 'sandy' in texture.

Add the egg yolks and the milk or water, work the mixture until it forms a good dough.

Roll into a ball and wrap in clingfilm and allow to rest for a good hour in a refrigerator.

You can also make the pastry in a food processor.

SAUCES, RELISHES AND VINAIGRETTES

Of all the culinary preparations people always seem baffled by sauces. The reason why chefs produce wonderful sauces is due to their experience and use of good natural ingredients which if treated with love and care will produce a lovely sauce. I use sauces very carefully and try to balance them with the main ingredient – fish or meat etc. Sauces must compliment a dish and never overpower it, they are greatly influenced by the quality of the ingredients and the way they are heated. Trial, error and failure are all part of the learning process.

I have given a few tips and as much guidance as I can in this chapter which should help you to improve your sauce-making skills. So have a go and enjoy yourselves. Remember cooking should be fun and not a chore.

RECIPES

BEURRE BLANC

SERVES 4

Ingredients

55g shallots – peeled and finely chopped
2 tbsps white wine vinegar
3 tbsps dry white wine
200g unsalted butter, diced
lemon juice
salt and freshly ground pepper

Preparation

In a small saucepan combine the shallots, vinegar and wine and boil until you have about 1 tablespoon of liquid. Add 2 tablespoons of cold water then, over a gentle heat, whisk in the cold diced butter a little at a time until completely amalgamated. The finished sauce will be creamy and homogenous and a delicate yellow.

CHEF'S TIP

If you add 2 tablespoons of cream after reducing the liquid it will prevent the sauce from separating.

HOLLANDAISE SAUCE
SERVES 4–6

Ingredients

1 tsp of pepper
1 tsp of vinegar
3 egg yolks
200 g butter – melted
Salt
Juice of half a lemon
cayenne pepper

Preparation

Mix together the pepper and vinegar with 3 tablespoons of water.
Heat and strain through a cloth into a warm bowl. Add the egg yolks
and beat thoroughly until the mixture has doubled in size. Bring the
hot butter to the boil and pour slowly onto the frothy egg mass,
whisking all the time. Add the salt, lemon juice and cayenne pepper
to taste.

WHITE WINE SAUCE

SERVES 4

Ingredients

20g shallots – chopped
10g butter
200ml fish stock
half a leek – chopped
150 ml dry white wine
30 ml Vermouth
200 ml double cream
100g butter – softened
salt
pepper – freshly ground

Preparation

Melt 10g of butter and sweat the shallots and leeks. Add the white wine, Vermouth and fish stock and reduce by two-thirds. Add the double cream and reduce again. Gradually whisk in the soft butter and season with salt and freshly ground pepper.

PRAWN SAUCE

MAKES 600ml

Ingredients

450g of prawn shells
1 onion
2 carrots
1 leek
2 sticks celery
1 tsp fennel seeds, crushed
1 tsp fresh tarragon
2 star anise, crushed
3 cloves garlic, finely chopped
200ml passata
150ml brandy and dry white wine
225ml double cream
salt and freshly ground pepper
a few drops of Pernod
55g unsalted butter
olive oil

Preparation

In a large pan heat the olive oil. Add the chopped vegetables, fennel
seeds, fresh tarragon and crushed star anise. Cook for 5 minutes.
Add the prawn shells and cook for 10 minutes. Add the white wine
and brandy and reduce by half. Add the passata and cook for a
further 5 minutes. Cover the prawn mixture with water and leave to
simmer for 25 minutes.

TOMATO AND BASIL VINAIGRETTE

SERVES 4

Ingredients

5 ripe tomatoes
2 medium shallots
2 garlic cloves
2 tbsps basil
salt
freshly ground pepper
1 tbsp good wine vinegar
1 tbsp lemon juice
125ml olive oil

Preparation

Prepare the vinaigrette. In a small bowl combine the tomatoes, shallots, garlic and basil. Season with salt and freshly ground pepper.

SPICY TOMATO VINAIGRETTE

SERVES 4–6 PEOPLE

Ingredients

125ml olive oil
1 tbsp red chilli
pinch of cayenne pepper, if needed
350 ml passatta
85 ml red wine vinegar
2 cloves garlic, finely chopped
half tsp salt
quarter tsp freshly ground pepper

Preparation

Warm the olive oil. Add the red chilli peppers. Leave to infuse for a few minutes over a low heat. Allow to cool to room temperature, then combine with remaining ingredients.

CHEF'S TIP

This is a wonderful vinaigrette and may be used to marinade goat's cheese. This quantity is sufficient to marinade 650g of mild goat's cheese cut into 6 rounds.

HERB VINAIGRETTE

Ingredients

150 ml olive oil
2 sprigs thyme
2 sprigs marjoram
2 basil leaves
1 sprig of parsley
2 tbsps white wine vinegar
70 ml cold water
salt and freshly ground pepper
half tsp caster sugar
1 clove of garlic – crushed

Preparation

In a saucepan combine the olive oil, garlic and herbs. Bring to the simmer and remove from the heat. Cover and leave to infuse at room temperature for 45 minutes. Pass through a fine sieve. Mix the vinegar, water and sugar together add the herb oil and season to taste. Whisk the vinaigrette before using.

TOMATO SAUCE

Ingredients

10–12 medium tomatoes
4 tbsps olive oil
half a medium onion – finely chopped
2 cloves garlic – peeled
1 large bay leaf
3 sprigs of parsley
2 sprigs thyme
1 tbsp chopped fresh basil
salt and sugar if desired
1 tbsp virgin olive oil or butter
freshly ground pepper

Preparation

Plunge the tomatoes into boiling water to remove the skins. Cut out the cores, and squeeze out the juice and seeds before chopping finely. Warm the olive oil, add the onion and the garlic cloves. After 30 seconds add the bay leaf, parsley and thyme and cook over a medium heat for 8–10 minutes, until the onion is soft. Add the tomatoes, raise the heat and continue to cook. After 5 minutes season with salt and cook until the sauce is no longer watery 10–12 minutes stirring occasionally.

Remove the herbs and garlic cloves. The finished sauce will retain some texture, but if you want a smooth sauce pass it through a food processor. Check the seasoning and stir in the basil and virgin olive oil or butter.

SALSA VERDE
(GREEN SAUCE)

Ingredients

1 bunch of chopped parsley
1 tbsp capers – rinsed and chopped
4 tbsps of onions or shallots – chopped
6 cloves of garlic – finely chopped
2 tbsps of anchovy – puréed or chopped
lemon juice or vinegar to taste
2 tbsps of breadcrumbs
30 ml fruity olive oil
salt and freshly ground pepper

Preparation

Combine all the ingredients – you may wish to add part of the vinegar/lemon juice and add the remainder to taste later. If you use the sauce for fish, you may omit the breadcrumbs.

PESTO SAUCE

This sauce is wonderful on top of grilled salmon or baked chicken.

Ingredients

1 bunch of basil leaves
2 tsps of finely chopped garlic
2 tbsps of pine nuts
half tsp of salt
half tsp freshly ground pepper
225 ml mild olive oil
85g Parmesan cheese – freshly grated

Preparation

Place all the ingredients except the olive oil and cheese into a blender or food processor and mix until combined. Add about half the olive oil and quickly purée before adding the remaining oil and processing to make a thick purée. Finally add the Parmesan cheese and check the seasoning. To store the pesto pour into a jar and film the top with a little olive oil to keep its bright green colour.

CHEF'S TIP

Why not try Asian pesto for something different with a spicy 'kick'. Just add some mint, coriander, 1 tablespoon chopped ginger 2 small green chillies and 2 large crushed cloves of garlic

SPICED CRANBERRY RELISH
SERVES 6–8 PEOPLE

Ingredients

zest and juice of 1 medium orange
225 ml red wine
350g cranberries
half medium onion – diced
25g fresh ginger – peeled and cut into julienne strips
3 tbsps of dark brown sugar
salt and freshly ground pepper
cinnamon – optional
2 tbsps Grand Marnier

Preparation

Cut the orange into julienne strips. Heat the juices in a small saucepan with a quarter of the wine and cook until tender – about 10 minutes.

In a medium saucepan, combine the cranberries, onion, rest of the wine, ginger, brown sugar, salt and pepper with the cinnamon and cook until the relish thickens, approximately 15–20 minutes, stirring occasionally.

Stir in the Grand Marnier and the reserved orange mixture. Cool and transfer to a serving bowl. Refrigerate until needed.

TRADITIONAL BREAD SAUCE
SERVES 6–8

Ingredients

450 ml milk
1 small onion
1 stick celery
1 bay leaf
3 cloves
1 sprig thyme
100 g white bread crumbs
salt and freshly ground pepper
nutmeg – freshly ground
25g butter
3 tbsps cream

Preparation

Place the milk, onion, celery, bay leaf and cloves in a small saucepan and bring to the boil. Cover and leave to infuse for 20 minutes. Strain, discarding the onion, celery and bay leaf. Return the milk to a clean pan. Bring back to the boil and add the bread crumbs and stir until the sauce thickens. Simmer for 2 minutes. Season well. Just before serving stir in the cream and butter.

CHOCOLATE SAUCE
MAKES 200ML

Ingredients

100g dark chocolate
150ml water
25g unsalted butter

Preparation

Break the chocolate into small pieces and melt in a small saucepan over a low heat, stirring occasionally.

Add the water and bring to the boil, stirring constantly and finally whisk in the butter.

RASPBERRY SAUCE

MAKES 280ML

Ingredients

315g raspberries
100g castor sugar
orange juice
lemon juice

Preparation

Purée the fruit with the sugar and force through a fine sieve. Taste
and enliven with lemon juice and orange juice.

Store in a covered container in the fridge. This sauce can be made
up to three days in advance.

CARAMEL SAUCE
MAKES 700ML

Ingredients

85ml water
100g sugar
500ml double cream

Preparation

Pour the water into a large saucepan and add the sugar. Cook the sugar until it turns a lovely brown colour. Take the pan off the heat immediately and beat in the cream.

Set the pan back on the heat and stir with a whisk until all the cream is mixed into the sugar.

Pass the sauce through a fine sieve into a bowl and keep in a cool place.

ORANGE SAUCE

Ingredients

2 eggs
140g castor sugar
225ml orange juice (freshly squeezed)

Preparation

Break the eggs into a bowl, add one-third of the sugar and whisk to a ribbon stage.

In a saucepan boil the orange juice with the remaining sugar, then pour the boiling juice on to the eggs, whisking continuously.

Pour the mixture into a pan and cook over a medium heat for 2 minutes. Pass the sauce through a sieve and leave to cool.

GINGER SAUCE
MAKES 600ML

Ingredients

85g fresh ginger root
300ml double cream
300ml milk
4 egg yolks
3 tbsps granulated sugar

Preparation

Peel the ginger and slice into rounds. Put the ginger in a saucepan and cover with water. Bring to the boil for 30 seconds. Drain well.

In a large saucepan, scald the cream, milk and blanched ginger. Remove from the heat and cover and stand for 30 minutes. Strain, discarding the ginger. Return cream to a saucepan.

In a bowl, beat together the egg yolks and sugar until the sugar has dissolved. pour about one fourth of the hot cream into the egg yolks whisking continuously. Return mixture to the saucepan and whisk in the rest of the cream. Cook over a low heat until the mixture thickens. Strain through a fine mesh strainer into a bowl.

Refrigerate when cool.

CHEF'S TIP

Scalding is bringing the milk or cream to the boil with the flavouring of your choice. Remove it from the heat and leave it with the lid on to cool and infuse, bringing out the best of the intense flavours.

STOCKS

Stocks are the foundation for all good sauces and are invaluable in the making of soups. Luckily for home cooks stock making does not have to be done daily.

Stocks may be prepared in advance, frozen in small plastic containers and used as needed. I urge you all to make stocks if you can for your sauces will certainly improve and once you have produced that first perfect sauce you will be hooked!

RECIPES

FISH STOCK
MAKES 1.4 LITRES

Ingredients

500 g fish bones (preferably whiting, sole or turbot)
1 onion – sliced
half leek – chopped
2 sticks of celery – chopped
1.5 ltr of cold water
2 bay leaves
parsley
50g butter

Preparation

Melt butter in a thick bottomed pan. Add the onions, leeks and celery and cook for 5 minutes. Add the well washed fish bones and the remainder of the ingredients. Bring to the boil, skim and simmer for 25 minutes before straining.

CHEF'S TIP

Never use Salmon bones or any oily fish for your stock or the stock will be oily. Try not to boil the stock or the fish bones will break up and make the stock cloudy and bitter.

COURT BOUILLON
MAKES 450ml

*Court bouillon translated into English means 'short broth'
and is a tasty stock for poaching or steaming fish or cooking lobster.*

Ingredients

1 small onion – peeled and chopped
1 carrot – washed and chopped
1 leek – washed and chopped
2 sticks of celery – washed and chopped
1 sprig fresh thyme
2 bay leaves
2 sprigs parsley
125 ml white wine
350 ml water
50ml white wine vinegar
1 tsp whole white pepper corns

Preparation

Tie the peppercorns and herbs together in a little bundle. Put the remaining ingredients into a saucepan and add the bundle or herbs. Bring to the boil then lower the heat and simmer for 20 minutes, skimming as necessary. Strain into a clean bowl and leave to cool. Refrigerate in a covered container for up to 3 days and use as needed.

CHICKEN STOCK

MAKES 4.5 LITRES

*I prefer to use chicken stock in recipes that
require a light flavoured stock.*

Ingredients

3.5kg chicken bones or boiling fowl
2 carrots – washed and chopped
2 large onions – peeled and chopped
4 sticks of celery including leaves – washed and chopped
2 bay leaves – crushed
2 leeks – split, washed and sliced
5.5ltr. of water

Preparation

Wash the chicken bones in cold water then put all the ingredients into a large stock pot and bring to the boil. Simmer for 2 hours. Skim any foam as it collects on top as this contains impurities that will cloud your stock. Remove from the heat when cooked and ladle the stock through a fine sieve. Leave to cool, then skim off the fat that has risen to the top. Refrigerate or freeze in small plastic containers.

CHEF'S TIP

*Use the same recipe but
use roasted turkey, duck
or pigeon bones for a very
different tasting stock.*

148

BEEF AND VEAL STOCK

MAKES 4.5 LITRES

Ingredients

3.5kg veal or beef bones
2 medium onions – roughly chopped
4 carrots – roughly chopped
2 sticks of celery – roughly chopped
1 leek – roughly chopped
225ml tinned plum tomatoes
6 cloves garlic crushed.
2 bay leaves
1 tsp salt and freshly ground black pepper
2 tbsps runny honey

Preparation

Pre-heat the oven to 190°C (375°F, Gas Mark 5). Roast the bones in a roasting pan for half an hour then pour over the honey, continue to cook for 1 hour turning to brown all sides. Transfer the bones and washed vegetables to a large stockpot. Pour off the fat from the roasting pan and de-glaze with 1.2 ltr of water, scraping any particles that stick to the bottom of the pan. Pour into the stock pot with enough water to cover the ingredients by 3 inches. Bring to the boil, reduce the heat to a slow simmer and cook without the lid for about 8 hours, skimming the foam as the impurities rise to the surface. More cold water may be added to keep the stock covered. Strain through a fine sieve, let cool then refrigerate of freeze.

CHEF'S TIP

This particular stock is invaluable in sauce making. The quantity it yields will last for months in the freezer and only takes a day to make. If you want a stronger stock reduce by half.

VEGETABLE STOCK

MAKES 2.4 LITRES

*At The Horn of Plenty I use this stock as the base for
most of my vegetarian dishes.*

Ingredients

450g onions – roughly chopped
2 large carrots
3 or 4 sticks of celery – cut into large chunks
55g (about 1 head) garlic
25g fresh ginger – peeled and sliced
1.5 tsps whole pepper corns
1 bay leaf
several large basil leaves
115g mushrooms – chopped
8 stalks of parsley

Preparation

In a large stock pot combine all the vegetables and sauté for
12–15 minutes, then add the water and herbs and simmer for 2
hours to extract all the juices.

If the stock is to be used for pasta or vegetable ragout reduce it
further to strengthen the flavour.

WEIGHTS AND MEASURES

5g	$^1/_8$ oz	115g	4 oz	400g	14 oz
10g	$^1/_4$ oz	125g	4 $^1/_2$ oz	425g	15 oz
15g	$^1/_2$ oz	140g	5 oz	450g	1lb
20g	$^3/_4$ oz	150g	5 $^1/_2$ oz	500g	1lb 2 oz
25g	1 oz	175g	6 oz	550g	1lb 4 oz
35g	1$^1/_4$ oz	200g	7 oz	600g	1lb 5 oz
40g	1$^1/_2$ oz	225g	8 oz	650g	1lb 7 oz
50g	1$^3/_4$ oz	250g	9 oz	700g	1lb 9 oz
55g	2 oz	275g	9$^1/_2$ oz	750g	1lb 10 oz
60g	2$^1/_4$ oz	280g	10 oz	800g	1lb 12 oz
70g	2$^1/_2$ oz	300g	10$^1/_2$ oz	850g	1lb 14 oz
75g	2$^3/_4$ oz	325g	11$^1/_2$ oz	900g	2lb
85g	3 oz	350g	12 oz	950g	2lb 2 oz
90g	3$^1/_4$ oz	375g	13 oz	1kg	2lb 4 oz
100g	3$^1/_2$ oz				

30ml	1fl oz	250ml	9fl oz	850ml	1$^1/_2$ pt
50ml	2fl oz	300ml	10fl oz	1 litre	1$^3/_4$ pt
75ml	2$^3/_4$fl oz	350ml	12fl oz	1.2 ltr	2 pt
100ml	3$^1/_2$fl oz	400ml	14fl oz	1.3 ltr	2$^1/_4$ pt
125ml	4 fl oz	425ml	15fl oz	1.4 ltr	2$^1/_2$ pt
150ml	5fl oz	450ml	16fl oz	1.5 ltr	2 $^3/_4$ pt
175ml	6fl oz	500ml	18fl oz	1.7 ltr	3 pt
200ml	7fl oz	600ml	1 pint	2 litres	3$^1/_2$ pt
225ml	8fl oz	700ml	1$^1/_4$ pt		

TEMPERATURE CONVERSIONS

°C	°F	Gas Mark	°C	°F	Gas Mark
110	225	$^1/_4$	190	375	5
120/130	250	$^1/_2$	200	400	6
140	275	1	220	425	7
150	300	2	230	450	8
160/170	325	3	240	475	9
180	350	4	250	500	10

INDEX

152